323
DISTURBING
FACTS
ABOUT OUR
WORLD

by

Nayden Kostov

323
DISTURBING
FACTS
ABOUT OUR
WORLD

by

Nayden Kostov

Luxembourg
2020

323 DISTURBING FACTS ABOUT OUR WORLD
first edition

Author: Nayden Kostov
Editor: Andrea Leitenberger
Format: 5,25 x 8

ISBN: 978-2-9199-602-3-1

CONTENTS

PROLOGUE

Following the success of my trivia website RaiseYourBrain.com, I published several award-winning compilations of hard-to-believe facts that have reached hundreds of thousands of readers. One of the chapters in each trivia book was "Disturbing Facts about Our World".

I decided to fill an entire volume with facts about upsetting crimes and mayhem, combined with unbelievable yet real instances of misfortune and misery. This is a book where grim examples of bigotry and hypocrisy are intertwined with amusing stories of bad luck. In the spirit of the times we live in, I dedicated a whole chapter to COVID-19 trivia and weird medical conditions. I am well aware that many potential readers might be overwhelmed by the condensed negativity, but hey... a fact is a fact! Continue to read if you are curious to learn:

- ❖ How can millipedes cause a train crash?
- ❖ What is the etymology of "thug"?

- Why were the trousers of New Zealand's farmers exploding?
- What is the depressing origin of the phrase "Hip Hip, Hooray"?
- Why did the Spanish Habsburgs royal family sleep with human mummies?
- Why was it legal in Iceland until 2015 to kill Basque people?
- Who was the "Deep Throat" informer from the Watergate scandal?
- How many people were killed trying to cross the notorious Berlin Wall?
- Why do snakes make a better pet than cats or dogs?
- What are the chances of getting killed by rubbish falling from space?
- How did polygamist men in Kuwait manage to visit all their wives during the coronavirus lockdown?

However incredible these pieces of trivia might sound, all entries have been verified and fact-checked.

CHAPTER I

COVID-19 trivia and weird medical conditions

1.

True *polycoria* occurs when you have two or more separate pupils in one eye. Each pupil will have its own, intact sphincter muscle and will individually constrict and dilate. This condition can affect your vision but is extremely rare.

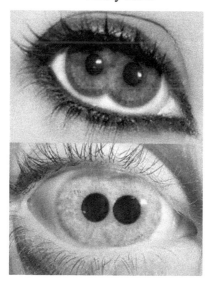

2.

In the USA, consumption of Corona beer dropped by more than 30% since the start of the 2020 pandemic of COVID-19, aka coronavirus.

3.

Kuwait's coronavirus lockdown created a logistical nightmare for polygamist men, who were facing jail time or substantial fines for leaving their homes to split time with all of their wives. Polygamist men were eventually granted more flexibility, allowing for those married to more than one woman to obtain electronic permits for one-hour visits twice a week.

4.

COVID-19 self-isolation in India is not easy – pushing people to self-isolate on trees, due to lack of space. The population density in India is 464 per km^2 (1,202 people per sq. mi).

5.

During the coronavirus shutdown in 2020, US professional gamblers in Las Vegas requested to be acknowledged as "independent contractors" and thus be able to claim unemployment payments while the casinos remained closed.

6.

In April 2020, during his daily White House briefing, US President Donald Trump suggested research into whether coronavirus might be treated by irradiating patients' bodies with UV light or by injecting disinfectant into the body. Many Americans misheard "ingestion of disinfectant", and in the following days, at least 100 people were admitted to hospitals after having swallowed various disinfectants.

7.

Coronavirus test kits used in Tanzania were declared faulty by President John Magufuli in April 2020. He said they had returned positive results on samples taken from a goat and a pawpaw fruit.
The samples had been secretly submitted to the labs as if taken from real people.

8.

A surgeon is three to four times as probable to be sued for medical malpractice as a psychiatrist is.

9.

In 1695, Margorie McCall had a fever and, believed to be dead, was buried by her family.

Soon after that, grave robbers, who regularly checked newly buried coffins, dug her up and tried to steal a valuable ring she was still wearing. The thieves could not remove the ring from her finger and proceeded to cut the finger off.

At this very moment, the woman awoke and the raiders fled terrified. She went straight home where her husband nearly died of shock.

Margorie lived many years after these events and even had another child before being buried again, this time forever.

10.

In March 2020, the terrorist organization ISIS issued a travel advisory for Europe to its fighters due to the then novel coronavirus pandemic, asking them to suspend travel to the region for terror attacks.

11.

In the very beginning of the COVID-19 lockdown in Malaysia, the Women and Family Ministry disseminated some advice for the ladies: "Do not nag your husband, do not be sarcastic when asking for help with the housework, and keep dressing nicely and wearing makeup."

The campaign was subsequently withdrawn.

12.

In 1962, the silicone breast implant was created, and the procedure was first performed on a woman in Texas, USA. Implants ruined the life and health of thousands of women and cost the manufacturers billions of dollars in punitive and compensatory damages. Many studies show that silicone breast implants are linked to certain autoimmune diseases, such as rheumatoid arthritis, Scleroderma, Sjörgen's syndrome, and Sarcoidosis. Additionally, side effects include scarring, breast pain, infections, sensory changes, leakage or rupture of the implant, bruising, bleeding, blood clots, skin necrosis, asymmetry, nipple discharge, calcium deposits, etc.

13.

In early 2020, amidst the COVID-19 pandemic, Thailand's controversial King Maha Vajiralongkorn, aka Rama X, decided to self-isolate in a posh hotel in the Alpine resort town of Garmisch-Partenkirchen, Germany. The 67-year-old king's entourage comprised a "harem" of 20 concubines and numerous servants.

14.

The royal family of Spanish Habsburgs were devout Catholics, known for their extensive collection of relics of saints, which were kept close to their bedrooms: many whole skeletons, over a hundred heads, and thousands of bones from all known saints.
Whenever someone from the royal family would fall ill, they would try to heal by bringing a mummy into their bed.

15.

Worldwide, smoking causes more than 7 million deaths per year.

16.

In the period 1890-1940, there were more incubators for prematurely born babies in amusements parks than there were in hospitals. For some reason, doctors were not impressed by these machines, maybe partially influenced by the eugenics theory that thrived at the time. Babies were displayed as an attraction and visitors paid money to see them. Desperate parents would bring their preemies in the hope that incubators would help their children survive. One of the most famous incubator-exhibit owners, Martin Couney, in fact strived to popularize the use of incubators. Couney claimed to have saved 6,500 babies over the course of his career and an overall 85% success rate.

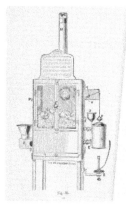

17.

Crash-test dummies were first used in the 1950s and, for many years, they were based around the 50th-percentile male. Today, the most commonly used dummy measures 1.77 m (5 ft 10 in) tall and weighs 76 kg (168 lb), i.e. considerably taller and heavier than an average woman. The dummy possesses both a male spinal column and male muscle-mass proportions, which, in turn, endanger female drivers. Men are more likely to be involved in a car crash and dominate the numbers of those seriously injured. However, when a woman has a car crash, she is 47% more likely to be seriously injured and 71% more likely to be moderately injured, even when factors such as height, weight, seatbelt usage, and crash intensity are taken into account.
Women are also 17% more likely to die.

18.

According to several studies, people with blue eyes have a higher tendency to abuse alcohol than people with darker eyes.

19.

Women tend to die from heart attacks more often than men. This is because most doctors are trained to look for symptoms, which, as it turns out, are typical for men but not always for women.

Women experience more often nausea, vomiting, and shortness of breath when they are suffering from heart disease, and during a heart attack, women are less likely to have the classic feeling of chest pain.

Often, they report a more subtle pressure or tightness, and not intense chest pain because their smaller arteries are more likely to be affected.

These differences may be the reason why doctors sometimes miss signs of heart distress in women.

20.

While text neck is not an official medical diagnosis, it is describing a repetitive stress injury where immoderate texting or smartphone use is believed to be the primary cause.

21.

In 2018, Ekaterina Fedyaeva, a 27-year-old Russian woman, lost her life during a botched routine surgery when she was virtually embalmed alive.
Doctors mistakenly administered a solution containing formaldehyde instead of a plain saline solution.

22.

The term Stockholm syndrome describes the phenomenon when hostages build a strong psychological connection with their captors during captivity.
The term was first used by journalists in 1973 when four people were held as hostages during a bank robbery in Stockholm, Sweden. After being released, the hostages tried to protect their captors and refused to testify in court against them.
In principle, emotional bonds between captor and captives are considered unreasonable in view of the danger experienced by the victims.
According to the FBI, about 8% of victims develop Stockholm syndrome.

23.

Women in the USA have one of the lowest life expectancies among any of the advanced countries. The life expectancy for women lags 2.5 years behind other high-income countries. Researchers cite the USA's lack of universal healthcare, relatively high child and maternal mortality rates, and high rates of homicides and obesity as contributing factors.

24.

In 2003, a study attempted to measure prescription dispensing accuracy in fifty pharmacies across six US cities. Researchers established that the error rate was almost 2% for the 4,481 prescriptions reviewed. They found seventy-seven mistakes, five of which were classified as "clinically important".

25.

There was a time when pet food in the UK was safer than hamburgers. Until 1989, hamburgers contained ground cattle offal and entrails, while pet food did not.

26.

US children get a quarter of their vegetables in the form of French fries.

27.

Before the discovery of penicillin, in 1928, syphilis was untreatable. It was a common practice for syphilis victims to cover their damaged noses with wooden prosthetic noses.

28.

Dr Chuck Gerba from the University of Arizona, USA, proved that there are 200 times more faecal bacteria on the average cutting board than on a toilet seat. Bacteria do not usually get there through contact with faeces, but rather with raw meat.

29.

Among pathogens, viruses are unique in their ability to infect all types of organisms: plants, animals, fungi, amoebas, bacteria, and even other viruses.

30.

Anatoli Petrovich Bugorski (born 1942), worked as a scientist at the Institute for High Energy Physics in Protvino, Russia. He used the most powerful Soviet particle accelerator, the U-70 synchrotron.

On 13 July 1978, a safety mechanism malfunctioned, and a 76 gigaelectronvolt proton beam pierced his skull. As he received what was thought to be a fatal dose of radiation, Bugorski was taken to a hospital where the doctors could observe his imminent demise. However, Bugorski survived and even completed his PhD.

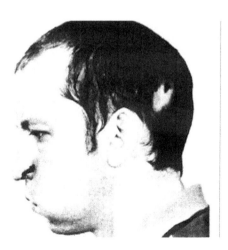
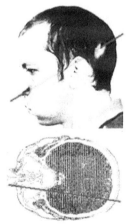

31.

Obesity has been recognised as a global epidemic by the World Health Organisation, followed by much empirical evidence to prove its infectiousness. If more people around you are obese, your own chances of becoming obese are also increased.

32.

According to several studies, measles infections in children can wipe out the immune system's memory of other illnesses such as influenza. This can leave kids who recover from measles vulnerable to other pathogens that they might have been protected from before their encounter with the measles virus.

33.

In 2013, a study linked a higher risk of diabetes to a Neanderthal gene mutation. Scientists think that the higher risk version of SLC16A11 gene was introduced through interbreeding between early modern humans and Neanderthals.

34.

According to a 2002 study, "Medical Errors and Wrong-Side Surgery - Orthopaedics", one out of every four orthopaedic surgeons with 25 years of experience has operated on the wrong limb.

35.

Thái Ngọc (born in 1942) is a Vietnamese insomniac, best known for his claim of being awake for more than 46 years as of this writing. Ngoc acquired the ability to live without sleep after an episode of fever in 1973, but according to the Vietnam Investment Review, there was no clear cause.

36.

According to a 2012 study of the North-Western University, USA, every time you remember an event from the past, your brain networks change. Thus, the next time you remember something, you might recall not the original event but what you remembered the previous time.

37.

In the 19ᵗʰ century, there were documented cases of
dental fillings literally exploding.

One of the most plausible explanations is that a badly
done filling offered the possibility of a build-up of
hydrogen within a tooth (due to the mixture of the metals
you have in the mouth, there might be spontaneous
electrolysis). One spark was enough to cause an
explosion.

38.

Few months after his bone marrow transplant,
Chris Long of Reno, Nevada (USA), found out that
the DNA in his blood had changed. It had all been
replaced by the DNA of his donor, a German man
he had never met.

Four years later, it was not just Long's blood that was
affected. Swabs of his lips and cheeks retrieved his DNA
along with that of his donor.

What is more, all of the DNA in his semen belonged to
his donor.

39.

A 2018 study, "Sleep duration and the risk of cancer: a systematic review and meta-analysis including dose-response relationship" (Chen, Y., Tan, F., Wei, L. et al.), could not prove a correlation between sleep duration and increased cancer risk. However, it indicated that short sleep duration increased cancer risk in Asians.

40.

Artificial intelligence can diagnose breast cancer more accurately than doctors can. In 2019, a team of scientists from Google Health and the Imperial College London, UK, fed a computer model with X-ray images from nearly 30,000 women.
The algorithm proved more efficient in reading mammograms than six experienced radiologists.

41.

A US study in 2014 found that people who felt unwell on the day of elections were more likely to favour attractive candidates than their less physically appealing opponents.

42.

In 2009, a 62-year-old man from Singapore was travelling to the USA to see relatives. He was detained after a routine fingerprint scan showed that he actually had none.

The man, reported in a medical journal case report only as "Mr S", had been on chemotherapy due to a head cancer. It was determined that the medicine, capecitabine, had provoked a hand-foot syndrome (aka chemotherapy-induced acral erythema), which is known to cause swelling and peeling on the palms and soles of the feet and, evidently, loss of fingerprints.

43.

Astronauts have long reported the strange feeling of seeing flashes while they are in space, even when their eyes remain closed.

It was established that the astronauts were "seeing" cosmic rays passing through their eyeballs.

Cosmic rays are high-energy particles with unknown origin.

44.

Photorhabdus luminescens (previously called *Xenorhabdus luminescens*) is a bioluminescent bacterium. It has been reported that infection by this bacterium in the wounds of soldiers in the American Civil War caused the wounds to glow, and that this aided the survival of the soldiers thanks to the production of antibiotics by *P. luminescens*. This led to the phenomenon's nickname "Angel's Glow".

45.

In 1895, the German company Bayer marketed diacetylmorphine as an over-the-counter drug under the trademark name Heroin. Its name was based on the German "*heroisch*", which means "*heroic; strong*".

Am. J. Ph.]   7   [December, 1901

BAYER Pharmaceutical Products

HEROIN–HYDROCHLORIDE

is pre-eminently adapted for the manufacture of cough elixirs, cough balsams, cough drops, cough lozenges, and cough medicines of any kind. Price in 1 oz. packages, $4.85 per ounce; less in larger quantities. The efficient dose being very small (1-48 to 1-24 gr.), it is

The Cheapest Specific for the Relief of Coughs

(In bronchitis, phthisis, whooping cough, etc., etc.)

WRITE FOR LITERATURE TO

FARBENFABRIKEN OF ELBERFELD COMPANY

SELLING AGENTS

P. O. Box 2160   40 Stone Street, NEW YORK

46.

In 1936, in India, as described by Nobel Laureate
Bernard Lown in "The Lost Art of Healing", a weird
experiment was conducted on a prisoner condemned to
die by hanging.

He was offered the possibility to choose an alternative –
to have his blood let out because this would be painless.
The victim agreed, was tied to the bed and blindfolded.

Hidden water containers were attached to the bed and
drip buckets put below. After few minor scratches were
made on his four limbs, the fake drip began: first rapidly,
then slowly, always loudly.

According to the story, when the dripping of water
stopped, prisoner's heart stopped too. That is to say, he
passed away without having lost a single drop of blood.

The physiological reactions of the "fight-or-flight"
response can kill instantly – there are numerous
confirmed cases of people dying of fright.

However, the so-called "parasympathetic rebound" can be life-threatening too: the body calms itself too much, and, in effect, stops the heart.

Voodoo deaths are also an example of the amazing power of the mind over the body.

47.

While only 2% of Europeans do not have the gene for smelly armpits, most East Asians and almost all Koreans lack it. That is why it could be hard to buy deodorant in South Korea.

48.

In 2004, a woman aged 43 gave birth in Gujarat, India, to her own grandchildren after "lending out" her womb to her daughter and son-in-law. The twin babies' parents, who live in Ilford, UK, had searched in vain for a surrogate mother for four years. The biological mother suffers from Rokitansky syndrome: while she has healthy ovaries and is able to produce embryos, her womb has not developed properly.

49.

During the early stages of the 2020 COVID-19 pandemic,
Luxembourg had one of the highest infection rates
per capita in the world. Yet, due to its well-developed
medical system, many beds in intensive care units
remained free and Luxembourg gallantly offered to look
after patients from neighbouring France.

50.

Many scientists have analysed the historical sources
describing the symptoms and claim that some of the
outbursts of the Plague were not caused by
bubonic plague, but rather by haemorrhagic fever.

51.

Speaking to your children from a very early age
stimulates them intellectually. Unfortunately,
many parents lack the time or simply do not understand
the need to do that. In a recent study in India,
it was established that poor people do not speak to
their children as much as rich people do.

52.

Historically, tomatoes were nicknamed "poison apple" and thought to be poisonous because a number of aristocrats got sick and died after eating them.
The truth was that wealthy Europeans used pewter plates, which were high in lead content.
Because tomatoes are very acidic, when placed on this particular tableware, they would extract lead from the plate, resulting in many deaths from lead poisoning.
No one made this connection between plate and poison at the time, and the tomato was blamed.

53.

After the COVID-19 lockdown, airlines started flying again. In late May 2020, a Eurowings flight made a roughly 1,200 km (730 mi) journey from Dusseldorf, Germany, to Olbia, Italy, but could not land as Olbia airport was closed, and had to go back to Dusseldorf.

54.

The European Monitoring Centre for Drugs and
Drug Addiction conducted a study on drug consumption
in 70 European cities.
They acquired pretty good data by just screening
wastewater for drugs.

55.

If you scare someone, they are more probable to comply
in the short-term. COVID-19 hysteria was
a good example.

56.

During the COVID-19 pandemic, a Russian nurse was
reprimanded for wearing only lingerie beneath a
see-through gown.

57.

In April 2020, Business Breakthrough (BBT) University
in Tokyo, Japan held a graduation ceremony
from distance.
Students remotely controlled avatar robots from their
homes. The avatar robots, dubbed "Newme", were
adorned in graduation caps and gowns for the ceremony,
complete with tablets showing the graduates' face.
BBT hoped the approach could be used as a model for
other schools wishing to avoid large gatherings amid the
COVID-19 pandemic.

58.

Snow cleaning patterns in most towns and
cities worldwide have been following the same approach
for decades: clean major roads first, particularly those
leading into and out of town, followed by smaller
local streets.

It turns out that these patterns benefit men and not so
much women. Men more frequently commute to and
from work, while many women drive all over to
run errands. Women also walk more, often pushing
a baby carriage as well.

In Sweden, several city councils have recently reversed
their approach, cleaning side roads and sidewalks first.
It had a huge impact, reducing the people admitted to
emergency centres, women in particular, and had a
corresponding economic impact from lower
healthcare costs.

Driving through 10 cm (4 in) of snow, as it turned out,
was less dangerous than walking through the snow.

CHAPTER II

True crime, bad decisions, and weird court cases

1.

Benjamin Schreiber is serving a life sentence in an Iowa, USA, prison for murder, but attempted to file an appeal for his release, arguing that he has already served his life sentence, despite spending less than 25 years behind bars until that moment. Schreiber had a remarkably interesting – and possibly unprecedented – argument. In 2015, nearly two decades into his sentence, Schreiber temporarily died and was brought back to life during a bout of severe septic poisoning. Since he was technically dead for a short period of time before he was revived, Schreiber argued that he had already served his life sentence. Unfortunately for him, the Iowa Court of Appeals ruled that the 66-year-old convicted murderer needs to stay in prison until he dies for good in order to fulfil his sentence.

2.

In 2018, Anna Mae Blessing, a 92-year-old woman from Arizona, USA, shot and killed her son, aged 72, in order to avoid being sent into a care home.

3.

Roberto Antonio "Cóndor" Rojas Saavedra (born 1957) is a retired Chilean football goalkeeper. In 1989, he deliberately injured himself during a World Cup qualifying match in an attempt to avoid a loss for the Chile national team. This ugly incident resulted in a lifetime ban for Rojas and one World Cup ban for Chile.

4.

In 2019, a Mexican judge permitted two people to use recreational cocaine.

They are now allowed to "possess, transport and use cocaine", but not to sell it.

5.

Paul Joseph Goebbels was the Minister of Propaganda of Nazi Germany from 1933 to 1945.

He was one of Adolf Hitler's closest aides.

To show his devotion, Goebbels named his six children after Hitler: Helga, Hildegard, Helmut, Holdine, Hedwig, and Heidrun (see photo).

6.

Three women from North Carolina, USA, were arrested in 2019 for organising fights between Alzheimer's and dementia patients. The nursing home employees encouraged patients to fight each other, recorded the fights and posted the videos on social media.

7.

Brian Douglas Wells (1956-2003) perished during a complex conspiracy involving a bank robbery, scavenger hunt, and improvised explosive device near Erie, Pennsylvania (USA). Wells, who was surrounded by police, died when an explosive collar locked to his neck detonated. The distressing incident known as the "collar bomb" or "pizza bomber" (because Wells was a pizza delivery man) was shown live on television. Wells's involvement in the plot is still a matter of controversy: whether he was innocent, or a knowing participant in the bank robbery, unaware that the bomb was real.

8.

In late 2019, a Nigerian pastor mistook petrol for holy water and unwittingly poured petrol over a parishioner, who was set alight by a nearby church candle at the Gloryland Estate on the outskirts of Lagos. The fire caused a nearby oil pipeline to explode, killing five more.

9.

Dry ice, which is frozen carbon dioxide, produces
a heavy vapour when put into water. In February 2020,
three people died after dry ice was poured
into a swimming pool during a birthday party in Moscow,
Russia. The victims were celebrating the birthday
of Instagram "influencer", Yekaterina Didenko,
at a pool complex in the Russian capital.
About 25 kg (50 lb) of dry ice were dropped into the pool
with the intention of creating a visual effect
to impress guests, but people inside the pool instantly
began to choke and lose consciousness.

10.

Edward Gingerich (1966-2011) was an Amish man
from Rockdale Township, Pennsylvania (USA).
He was the first Amish person to be convicted
of homicide.
In 1993, he brutally murdered his wife in front of their
children yet was only sentenced to five years in prison.

11.

On 23 May 2018, four US teens snuck into school
before graduation and sprayed racist and
homophobic graffiti.

Wearing masks, Seth Taylor, Tyler Curtiss, Joshua
Shaffer, and Matthew Lipp committed the vandalism at
night on the Glenelg High School campus
in Glenwood, Maryland.

While cameras did not capture their faces, their cell
phones automatically connected to the campus Wi-Fi
thus recording their individual student IDs.

12.

Emmanuel Nwude is a Nigerian con man and former
Director of Union Bank of Nigeria. He is notorious for
having defrauded Nelson Sakaguchi, a Director at
Brazil's Banco Noroeste, of $242 m (€210 m) between
1995 and 1998.

Nwude posed as Paul Ogwuma, then Governor of the
Central Bank of Nigeria, and successfully convinced

Sakaguchi to "invest" in a imaginary new airport near the nation's capital, Abuja, in exchange for a $10 million commission.

In 1997, the Spanish Banco Santander intended to take over the Banco Noroeste Brazil. The fraud was uncovered after a joint board meeting, when a Santander employee requested additional information regarding a large sum of money, 40% of Noroeste's total value, sitting in the Cayman Islands. This triggered criminal investigations in Brazil, the United Kingdom, Nigeria, Switzerland, and the United States.

To secure the sale to Santander, the owners of Banco Noroeste, paid the missing millions themselves. Eventually, Banco Noroeste collapsed in 2001.

13.

In early 2020, France's competition and fraud watchdog, DGCCRF, imposed a fine of €25 m ($27 m) on Apple for deliberately slowing down older iPhone models without making it clear to consumers.

14.

The 1992 Los Angeles Riots took place in Los Angeles County, USA, in the period 29 April – 4 May 1992.

Everything began in Los Angeles, after a jury acquitted four police officers for use of excessive force in the arrest and beating of Rodney King, which had been videotaped and widely broadcast on TV.

Widespread looting, assault, arson, and murder took place during the riots, which local police was unable to control.

The California Army National Guard, the United States military, and numerous federal law enforcement agencies had to intervene.

The aftermath was gruesome: 63 people had been killed, 2,383 people had been injured, more than 12,000 had been arrested, and estimates of property damage were over $1 billion.

It is noteworthy that not a single McDonald's restaurant was damaged.

15.

In September 1986, citizens of Cleveland, Ohio (USA), tried to beat the world record by releasing 1.5 million balloons. It was quite a spectacle until bad weather brought the balloons back over the city, disrupting traffic, grounding planes, and most likely causing two deaths: tragically, two people died when Coast Guard's rescue helicopters were unable to reach their overturned boat.

16.

As of 2015, Telford was the UK's city with the highest rate of sex crimes against children.

17.

The 1984 Rajneeshee bioterror attack was the food poisoning of 751 people in The Dalles, Oregon (USA), through the contamination of salad bars at ten local restaurants with salmonella. A group of followers of Bhagwan Shree Rajneesh (later known as Osho), led by Ma Anand Sheela, had conspired to incapacitate the voting population of the city so that their own candidates would win the 1984 Wasco County elections.
This incident was the first and is the largest bioterrorist attack in the American history.

18.

The Bonnot Gang (La Bande à Bonnot) was a French criminal gang that was active in France and Belgium during the so-called Belle Époque, from 1911 to 1912. The group used cutting-edge technology (including cars and automated rifles) not yet available to the French police.
They pioneered in using a getaway car on 14 December 1911 in France.

19.

Michael Hubert Kenyon (born in 1944) is a US criminal nicknamed the Enema Bandit. He pleaded guilty to a series of armed robberies of female victims, some of which involved sexual assaults in which he would give them enemas. He is also known as the "Champaign Enema Bandit", the "Ski Masked Bandit", and "The Illinois Enema Bandit". In December 1975, he pleaded guilty to six counts of armed robbery and was given six to twelve years in prison for each count, but was never charged for the enema assaults. He was paroled in 1981 having served only six years.

20.

Spencer Perceval KC (1762-1812) was a British politician who served as Prime Minister of the United Kingdom from 1809 until his assassination. Perceval is the only British Prime Minister to have been murdered. He was also the only UK Attorney General to become Prime Minister.

21.

William I, Prince of Orange (1533-1584) – aka William the Silent, William the Taciturn, or William of Orange – was the main leader of the Dutch Revolt against the Spanish Habsburgs that started the Eighty Years' War (1568-1648) and resulted in the formal independence of the United Provinces of the Netherlands in 1581.
He was the first head of state to be assassinated by a handgun.

22.

In August 2019, NASA started investigating the first allegation of a crime committed in space.
A bitter separation of a same-sex couple involving the astronaut, Ms Anne McClain, and Ms Summer Worden led to an unusual accusation: McClain was accused of improperly accessing Worden's bank account from the International Space Station.
In April 2020, McClain was cleared of all charges. Her ex-spouse, a 44-year-old former Air Force intelligence officer, faces up to five years in prison for perjury.

23.

Deep web and dark web are not the same thing, although they can overlap significantly.

The deep web refers to all the pages that are not indexed, meaning that most search engines will not return them to you after a search. Their crawlers do not "see" these pages, making them de facto invisible. To access one of these pages, you need to know their exact address or follow a link. It is noteworthy that the deep web can include significant parts of the legitimate, mainstream web (for instance Amazon pages), simply because they are personalized for users and not all URLs are meant to be indexed.

The dark web is a layer even deeper – technically also part of the deep web (which makes it inaccessible unless you know exactly where to go), but focused on illegal activities and services. While a section of the illegal content can be well-meant (for instance, Wikileaks documents or scanned rare books), the rest is simply a gruesome and appalling marketplace for drugs, weapons, child pornography, or even for hiring hitmen.

24.

Many tourists visiting Medellin, Colombia, take the opportunity to learn more about Pablo Escobar, but locals do not like the idea of companies offering tours that glorify the notorious drug lord.

One of the tours includes a meeting with Roberto Escobar (Pablo's brother), who had a bounty of $10,000,000 on his head and served time in prison.

At the end of this tour, tourists have a coffee with him, take selfies and inquire in broken Spanish about life back in the time with Pablo.

25.

In 2007, Saudi Arabia defended a controversial verdict sentencing a 19-year-old gang-rape victim to 200 lashes and six months in jail.

The Shi'ite Muslim woman, raped in 2006 by seven men, was found guilty of "violating Saudi Arabia's rigid Islamic Sharia law on segregation of the sexes".

26.

In 2019, Marshae Jones was five months pregnant when she was shot in the stomach. Her foetus did not survive the shooting, which the authorities say happened during a dispute with another woman, Ebony Jemison. However, it was Ms Jones who was charged in the death "because she started the fight that led to the shooting and failed to remove herself from harm's way".
Ebony Jemison was not indicted.

27.

In the USA, 1939 was the so-called Year of Goldfish Gulping. It started out with one live goldfish, swallowed up by a Harvard freshman on a dare.
Three weeks later it rose to three, and four days after that, the number of goldfish swallowed jumped to 24. By the end of April 1939, the record was 101.
Students at colleges across the country had participated the unsettling quest to see how many live goldfish a single person could swallow
in one sitting.

28.

The Holden-Keating Gang was a bank-robbing group led
by Thomas James Holden (1896-1953) and
Francis Keating (1899-1978).

Holden was described by a spokesperson for the FBI as
"a menace to every man, woman and child in America"
and was the first fugitive to be officially listed on the
FBI's Top Ten Most Wanted List on 14 March 1950.
Thanks to his widely publicised picture, he got arrested
fifteen months later and imprisoned for life.

1. Thomas James Holden

2. Morley Vernon King

3. William Raymond Nesbit

4. Henry Randolph Mitchell

5. Omar August Pinson

6. Lee Emory Downs

7. Orba Elmer Jackson

8. Glen Roy Wright

9. Henry Harland Shelton

10. Morris Guralnick

29.

Joseph "Mad Dog" Taborsky (1924-1960) was a murderer who was given the death penalty after a series of brutal robberies and murders in Connecticut, USA, during the 1950s.

Six people were killed during these events, which became known as the "Mad Dog Killings".

To date, Taborsky is the only US convict sent to death row twice for different crimes.

He first came to Connecticut's death row in 1950 for a murder during a robbery. His younger brother, Albert, testified against him at the trial in exchange for a life sentence.

In prison, Albert showed signs of mental disorder and was institutionalized. Joseph Taborsky appealed his case and, in 1955, the Connecticut Supreme Court reversed his death sentence because the only witness against him was deemed insane.

He quickly accumulated new robberies and murders and, in 1957, was sentenced again to die in the electric chair.

30.

Giles Corey (1611-1692) was an English-born
American farmer who was accused of witchcraft
along with his wife, Martha Corey, during
the Salem Witch Trials.

After being arrested, Corey refused to enter a plea of
guilty or not guilty. The law at the time stipulated that a
person who refused to plead could not be tried.

To avoid people cheating justice, the legal remedy for
refusing to plead was "*peine forte et dure*" (a medieval
form of torture in which the body was pressed with
heavy weights). Prisoners were stripped naked, and heavy
boards were placed on their bodies. Then rocks were laid
on the planks until they would plead or would die.

Corey remained the only example of such a sanction in
American history – and died after three days of
this torture.

31.

On average, US police forces killed three people per day
in 2019, for a total of nearly 1,100 killings.

32.

The Angel Makers of Nagyrév were a group of women from the village of Nagyrév, Hungary, who in the period 1914-1929 poisoned to death over 300 people. Susanna Fazekas, the local midwife, supplied them with arsenic.
As there was no doctor in the village and Fazekas's cousin was responsible for filling the death certificates, murders went undetected for years.

33.

Branding as a form of punishment and a mark of ownership has a long history.
In antiquity, Greeks and Romans branded slaves and runaways by stamping the skin with hot irons.
In England during the 1500s, King Edward VI decreed gypsies and vagabonds could be branded with a "V" on the chest.
Branding was abolished in 1829 with the sole exception of army deserters. Until 1879, when the practice was totally abandoned, the mark was tattooed on the body.

34.

In 2019, James Gilbert Kwarteng of Palma de Mallorca, Spain, was accused of scamming Amazon out of about €300,000, or nearly $370,000.

His method was surprisingly simple: order the goods, send back the boxes filled with dirt the same weight as the product, and keep the valuable merchandise. Amazon's policy is to refund when a customer makes a claim and returns a package.

The issue was that the company did not immediately open the packages upon receipt and would weigh them instead. Their procedure has since changed.

35.

Two UK twins who were separated at birth married each other without realising they were brother and sister. As the couple had no idea they were blood relatives until after their wedding, the High Court annulled their marriage in 2008. The pair had been separated soon after birth and each was adopted by a different family. Neither was told they had a twin.

36.

The Radium Girls were US factory workers who contracted radiation poisoning while painting watch dials with self-luminous paint.

The painting was performed by women at three different United States Radium factories from 1917 to 1926.

The women had been told the paint (made from powdered radium, gum arabic, and water) was harmless.

They unwittingly ingested deadly amounts of radium after being instructed to "point" their brushes on their lips in order to give them a fine tip.

Some workers even painted their fingernails, face, and teeth with the glowing substance.

37.

In 2016, a spelling mistake in an online bank transfer instruction helped partially prevent a $1-billion (about €900 million) heist involving the Bangladesh Central Bank and the New York Federal Reserve. Unknown criminals hacked Bangladesh Bank's systems and stole its credentials for payment transfers. Then they sent to the Federal Reserve Bank of New York dozens of requests for money transfers from the Bangladesh Bank's account there to entities in the Philippines and Sri Lanka. Four transfers for a total of $81 million went through, while a fifth, for $20 million, to a Sri Lankan non-profit organization was blocked because the hackers misspelled the name of the NGO, Shalika Foundation.

Hackers misspelled *"foundation"* in the NGO's name as *"fandation"*, prompting the intermediary bank, Deutsche Bank, to request clarification from the Bangladesh Central Bank, which stopped the payment.

38.

Also known as the Original Night Stalker and the East Area Rapist, the Golden State Killer is suspected of committing 51 rapes and 12 murders in California, USA, between 1974 and 1986. In 2018, police arrested 72-year-old Joseph James DeAngelo in Citrus Heights, California, in connection with the crimes.

The police used the genealogy website GEDmatch to solve the case. Comparing decade-old crime scene DNA to profiles on genealogy websites led investigators to relatives of the suspect.

39.

Rodney James Alcala (born in 1943) is a US convicted rapist and serial killer who was sentenced to death in California for five murders committed in that state between 1977 and 1979.

Alcala is also dubbed the "Dating Game Killer" because of his 1978 appearance on the TV show The Dating Game in the midst of his murder mayhem.

40.

David P. Baugh is one of the most respected and experienced criminal trial lawyers in the Commonwealth of Virginia, USA. In 1998, he represented Ku Klux Klan member Barry Elton Black, prosecuted for burning a cross at a KKK rally in Virginia. The case ended up in the US Supreme Court where Black's conviction was overturned. The irony here is that Mr Black is a white supremacist, while his attorney, Mr Baugh, is African American.

41.

In 2018, the High Court in Rajasthan, India, overturned a conviction of murder. Kumari Chandra, a 21-year-old woman, was accused of pushing three children into a well. While two of them were rescued, one boy drowned. She claimed she had been influenced by Premenstrual Stress Syndrome.
The High Court accepted Chandra's defence and acquitted her on the ground that "she acted under a defect of reason owing to a disease of the mind".

42.

In 2011, Nancy Crampton Brophy, wrote the essay, "How to Murder Your Husband", outlining how to kill your spouse and get away with the crime. In 2018, she was arrested for killing her own husband and, as of this writing, is still awaiting her trial in jail.

43.

In 2016, an Egyptian military court made a mistake by sentencing a four-year-old boy to life in prison for murder. Ahmed Mansour Qurani Ali was indicted along with 115 others in connection with riots by Muslim Brotherhood supporters in Fayoum province in 2014. At the time of the events, he was one year old.

44.

Every six months, more US citizens commit suicide or are murdered than have died in the last 25 years in terrorist attacks and the wars in Iraq and Afghanistan combined.

45.

In 1987, a German teenager landed a small airplane
(see photo) on the Red Square, near the Kremlin.
Mathias Rust (born 1968) is a German amateur aviator
known for his illegal flight to Moscow, Soviet Union.
Rust claimed that he wanted to create an "imaginary
bridge" to the East, and that his flight was intended to
ease tension and suspicion between
the two Cold War sides.
Rust's flight through a purportedly impenetrable air
defence system had a great impact on the Soviet military
and led to the dismissal of numerous senior officers,
including the Minister of Defence, Marshal of
the Soviet Union Sergei Sokolov, and the Commander-in-
Chief of the Soviet Air Defence Forces,
Chief Marshal Alexander Koldunov.
For violation of border crossing and air traffic laws, and
for provoking an emergency upon his landing, Rust was
sentenced to four years in Soviet prison, of which he
served fourteen months.

46.

Hans Schmidt (1881-1916) illegally married,
impregnated, and then brutally murdered and
dismembered his mistress.

For that crime, he was eventually executed via
electrocution, and to this day is the only Catholic priest
ever executed in the United States.

47.

A former US master sergeant, Timothy Hennis, has been sentenced to death, acquitted and convicted again for the same crime. In 1986, he was sentenced to death by a civilian court for three murders, acquitted in an appeal and then sent back to death row decades later for the same crimes by a military court, thanks to DNA evidence.

48.

Sakigake Watanabe was a Japanese criminal who escaped from prison, took a new identity and became a judge in 1887. The problem was that he took a job in Nagasaki, the very same court where he had been sentenced.
In 1891, the prosecutor who had handled his embezzlement trial recognized Watanabe and the fugitive was sent back to prison. Watanabe's deeds attracted vast attention and won the sympathy of many people. Thanks to the public pressure, he was pardoned the year after.

49.

24-year-old Yee Xiong was a victim of sexual assault in 2012. The attacker, 26-year-old Lang Her, was not convicted of rape; instead, he pleaded no contest to felony assault and was sentenced to one year in prison. In 2016, Mr Her sued Ms Xiong for calling him a "rapist" in an interview.

50.

In February 2020, the police of Osaka, Japan, arrested Hiroaki Suda for stealing two bike seats. It turned out that he had stolen almost 6,000 seats in the course of twenty-five years "to relieve stress at work and, gradually, collecting them turned out to be fun".

51.

In late 2019, Akitoshi Okamoto, a 71-year-old man from Tokyo, Japan, was arrested for making 24,000 complaint calls to his phone operator's free number over two years.

52.

The Watergate scandal was a highly publicized political scandal involving the administration of
US President Richard Nixon from 1972 to 1974 that ultimately led to Nixon's resignation.
The scandal erupted from the Nixon administration's attempts to cover up its involvement in the botched break-in of the Democratic National Committee headquarters at the Washington DC Watergate Office Building on 17 June 1972.
Deep Throat is the pseudonym assigned to the secret informant who provided information in 1972 to The Washington Post, including details about the involvement of Nixon's administration.
In 2005, thirty-one years after Nixon's resignation and eleven years after Nixon's death, it was revealed that former FBI Deputy Director, William Mark Felt Sr., was Deep Throat.
By the way, Deep Throat was named after a porn movie.

53.

In 2004, partygoers on Lake Travis, Texas (USA),
apparently hoping to catch a glimpse of naked
sunbathers, crowded on one side of a floating barge close
to a nudist beach. This prompted the ship to capsize and
dump all sixty people into the lake.
Two people suffered minor injuries.

54.

In 2014, British Jane Mulcahy attempted to sue
her former lawyers for professional negligence, claiming
that, alongside several other allegations, they failed to
advise that finalising divorce proceedings
would inevitably cause her marriage to end.
The curious case was rejected by the court.

55.

In May 2020, a five-year-old US boy was pulled over by
Utah police while driving his parents' car
"to California to buy a Lamborghini".
The boy had $3 in his pocket.

56.

Japanese police officers and shop owners use colour balls
to mark runaway thieves and cars.

The orange spheres are called *"bohan yo kara boru"*
(*anticrime colour balls*).

Basically, they are paintballs – plastic orbs filled with a
brightly-coloured liquid pigment. However, unlike the
fun variety, these balls are kept on hand by shop owners
in case of a holdup.

The idea is to throw one after a robber and mark them,
thus improving the chance of an arrest. The advice is
to aim for the ground near the perpetrator's feet, because
the balls shatter on impact and release their contents in
a radius as wide as 10 m (33 ft), or fling onto the getaway
vehicle, since a car or motorbike offers a larger target.
Even if the balls are not actually used, the mere fact that
they are in the store and visible to would-be thieves
helps protect the store, according to
the Tokyo Metropolitan Police.

(see picture)

57.

In 2016, a film being shot at Malta airport about a plane hijacking was disrupted by the real hijacking of a Libyan Airbus A320. The movie – Entebbe – is based on a hostage situation that occurred in 1976 in Uganda. Then, Israeli forces freed 105 hostages in a surprise raid at Uganda's Entebbe airport, killing eight hostage-takers and twenty Ugandan troops.

Unlike the 1976 hijacking, the two hijackers in 2016 incident surrendered peacefully to Maltese police.

58.

In one instance, the heavy-metal band, Iron Maiden, planned the route for their tour based on where their music is most pirated. They hired a company to explore the deep web for torrent activity of fans who downloaded the band's albums without paying.

59.

Elon Reeve Musk FRS (born 1971) is the founder, CEO and chief engineer/designer of SpaceX; co-founder, CEO and product architect of Tesla, Inc.; founder of The Boring Company; co-founder of Neuralink; and co-founder and initial co-chairman of OpenAI. He was ranked joint-first on the Forbes list of the Most Innovative Leaders of 2019 and the 23rd richest person in the world. Musk is not immune to some not so wise decisions, though. In 2018, he smoked weed live on a popular podcast and Tesla's stock price dropped. The same year, Musk was sued by the US Securities and Exchange Commission for a tweet claiming that funding had been secured for potentially taking Tesla private.

Another 2018 tweet contained a random unsubstantiated insult, "pedo guy". In May 2020, he tweeted that Tesla's share price was too high, sending its shares down. Along with that, he announced the birth of his son, trying to name him X Æ A-12. The name was deemed illegal under California law because it contained characters that are not in the modern English alphabet and the child was eventually named "X AE A-XII", with "X" as a first name and "AE A-XII" as a middle name.

60.

In 2016, the then 18-year-old Izaha Akins arrived at Mohawk High School in Sycamore, Ohio (USA).
He claimed to be a newly elected state senator who had been appointed to replace Republican Senator Dave Burke as the guest speaker.
No one suspected foul play until one month later.
Akins told the police: "They could easily have Googled me".

61.

Alcatraz Island (aka Alcatraz or The Rock) was a maximum-security federal prison 2 km (1.2 mi) off the coast of San Francisco, USA, which was in use from 1934 to 1963.

Unlike other prisons, inmates were always offered hot showers. Why would the authorities do that?

They believed it would deter prisoners from trying to escape by swimming in the cold waters around the island.

62.

In 1903, an inmate named Will West arrived at the prison in Leavenworth, Kansas (USA), and inadvertently helped spread the use of fingerprints. The prison's clerks were astonished to realise that he was a doppelgänger of another inmate, similarly named William West. No one was able to distinguish them; even their body measurements were identical. Today, DNA testing and biometrics, such as retinal scans, have also become standard tools for identifying people.

However, fingerprinting remains a practical tool for law enforcement, and was at the time the only way to tell apart the two Wests.

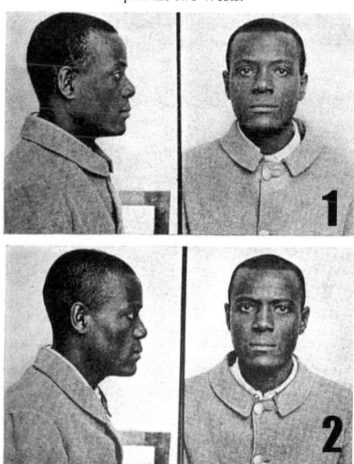

63.

The words "*con man*" and "*con artist*" derive from "*confidence man*". A famous swindler named William Thompson was operating in New York, USA, in the 1840s.

When he eventually got arrested and put on trial for his cheating, the newspapers mockingly called him "The Confidence Man". The name quickly became generic for any swindler, got shortened to "*con man*", and gave rise to related words like "*con game*", "*short con*", "*long con*", and simply "*con*".

64.

In 2016, Albanian police purchased electric cars. However, at the time, there were no recharging spots at Albanian fuel stations or around Albanian cities, so the cars had to head back to the police stations to be recharged every day or twice a day.

The estimated range of the purchased Volkswagen e-Golf varied between 130 and 190 kilometres (80-118 miles).

65.

Un ballo in maschera (A Masked Ball) is an 1859 opera in three acts by Giuseppe Verdi.

The plot is based on a real event: the assassination in 1792 of King Gustav III of Sweden, shot as a result of a political conspiracy while attending a masked ball, dying of his wounds thirteen days later.

66.

According to the Guinness Book of Records, the largest speeding fine is a reported $290,000 (€260,000) ticket given to an anonymous Swiss motorist who was caught driving 137 km/h (85 mph) in an 80 km/h (50 mph) zone in a village near St. Gallen, Switzerland, in January 2010.

He was driving a Ferrari and the fine was calculated based on his wealth, which the court assessed at $22.7 million (€20 million).

67.

In December 2019, Italian artist, Maurizio Cattelan, went viral for duct-taping a banana to a wall and selling it for more than €100,000 ($120,000). A few days later, performance artist, David Datuna, took a bite of that action by plucking the six-figure fruit off the wall, peeling it, and literally eating it in front of dumbfounded onlookers. He called his performance "Hungry Artist".

(see photo)

68.

Ferdinand Waldo Demara (1921-1982), aka "The Great Impostor", masqueraded as a great number of people: a naval surgeon, a civil engineer, a sheriff's deputy, an assistant prison warden, a doctor of applied psychology, a hospital orderly, a lawyer, a child-care expert, a Benedictine monk, a Trappist monk, an editor, a cancer researcher, and a teacher.

He served as a trauma surgeon aboard HMCS Cayuga, a Royal Canadian Navy destroyer during the Korean War. He improvised successful major surgeries and prevented infections with generous amounts of penicillin.

His most remarkable surgical practices were performed on sixteen Korean combat casualties who arrived at the same time. While the patients were being prepared for surgery, Demara went to his room to speed-read a textbook on general surgery and performed various surgeries, including major chest surgery. Nobody died as a result of Demara's surgeries.

To avoid the embarrassment of having allowed an impostor into its ranks, Canadian officials chose not to press charges. Instead, Demara was quietly dismissed from the Royal Canadian Navy.

CHAPTER III

Bigotry and hypocrisy, mixed with upsetting past events

1.

The actress Gwyneth Paltrow marketed a scented candle named "Smells Like My Vagina".

2.

People for the Ethical Treatment of Animals (aka PETA) position themselves as a "pro-animal" organisation. Numerous pieces of evidence surfaced however, that in Virginia, USA, PETA had euthanized the overwhelming majority of dogs and cats that it accepted into its shelters.

3.

In 2011, the US Congress passed a bill allowing, when composing a school lunch, a pizza with two tablespoons (30 mL) of tomato paste to qualify as a vegetable.

4.

In 2016, Saudi Grand Mufti Sheikh Abdulaziz Al-Sheikh declared playing of chess "forbidden".

5.

The Berlin Wall was an extensive concrete wall that physically and ideologically divided Berlin, Germany, from 1961 to 1989.

German Democratic Republic (aka East Germany, or GDR) started the construction on 13 August 1961.

The Wall separated West Berlin from surrounding East Germany, including East Berlin.

The barrier included multiple guard towers, accompanied by a wide area (later known as the "death strip") that contained anti-vehicle trenches and beds of nails.

The Eastern Bloc justified the Wall as protecting its population from fascist elements "conspiring to prevent the "will of the people" from building a socialist state in East Germany".

It is estimated that 511 people were killed while attempting to flee to West Berlin over the Wall by East Germany's border guards.

6.

In Victorian England, having all your teeth removed was considered the perfect gift for a 21st birthday or a newly married bride.

7.

Until the early 20th century, Korean women almost never heard their names.
They were referred to as "the wife of...", "the sister of", "the mother of", etc.

8.

The Radboud University in Nijmegen, the Netherlands, offers its students an unorthodox way to cope with stress. They dug a grave, in which students could lie and reflect on the transience of life and, allegedly, combat stress.

9.

In 2018, China banned Hip-Hop culture and tattoos from television.

10.

"Negre" (literally *"Negro"*) used to mean *"ghost-writer"* in French until a few years ago.

Now the term used is *"prête-plume"*, literally *"borrowed pen"*.

11.

Tiktok, the Chinese-owned short-video-sharing app popular with teens, instructed moderators to suppress posts created by users deemed too ugly, poor, or disabled for the platform.

12.

In 2018, a 32-year-old US woman, Lauren Cutshaw, was arrested after speeding through a stop sign.

She became famous for having asked the police to let her off because she is "a clean, thoroughbred white girl".

13.

In many US states, it is still legal to leave children unattended in a car.

14.

In September 2019, Kenyan MP Lilian Achieng Gogo proposed a law persecuting people who fart on airplanes. In her opinion, it was causing "discomfort and insecurity" on flights. This proposal came just a month after a fart accident created turmoil in a local Kenyan legislature. A member of the Homa Bay County Parliament passed gas in such a manner that the Speaker had to suspend the debate and evacuated the MPs for few minutes.

15.

The US Women's football (soccer) team won the last World Cup, while the men's team did not even qualify for Russia 2018. Yet, female players earn significantly less than male players do. Twenty-eight women's national team players filed a lawsuit over equal pay. The lawyers of the US football governing body justified the payment gap, stating that the job of a male footballer on the national team "requires a higher level of skill based on speed and strength" than their female counterparts.

16.

The Cherry Hill school district in New Jersey, USA, passed a policy in 2019 that prohibits high school students who owe $75 or more in meal payments from "participating in extracurricular activities, purchasing tickets for school dances, including proms, attending class trips, including the Senior Trip, and purchasing a yearbook".

17.

Numerous studies proved that people tend to feel more at ease with people from their race and/or religion.
For instance, in the United States of America black people trust doctors of the same race more and if their family doctor is black, they on average live longer. In the same vein, US black students with a black teacher show better school results and are less likely to drop out of school.
In India, bank clients who share the same religion with the bank teller are proven to default on their loans less often.

18.

Shindo Renmei was a secret organization of Brazilian-Japanese nationalists who claimed Japan had won World War II and would assassinate those who would not agree. It was disbanded around 1955.

19.

Still today, both German phrases *"Mit deutschem Gruß"* (*with German greetings*), a written equivalent to *"Heil Hitler"*, and *"Unsere Ehre heißt Treue"* (*our honour is called loyalty*), the slogan of the SS, are illegal to say or write in Germany and Austria.

20.

Ever wondered where the phrase "Hip Hip, Hooray" comes from? This phrase, often chanted at celebrations, have been used also in Nazi Germany.

It derives from the Latin battle cry, *"Hieroslyma est perdita"* (*Jerusalem is fallen*). When fighting Jewish people, Germanic tribes used a variation, *"Hep Hep Huraj"*, which roughly translates to *"Jerusalem is fallen and we are on the way to paradise"*.

"Hep Hep" was the rallying cry used in the so-called Hep Hep Riots – the violent riots aimed at German Jews in the 19th century.

Gradually, it evolved to hip hip hooray and lost this negative association.

21.

Saint Vitus was a Christian saint from Sicily, Italy. He died as a martyr during the persecution of Christians by co-ruling Roman Emperors Diocletian and Maximian in 303 CE. St Vitus is honoured as the patron saint of actors, dancers, and epileptics.

22.

Saint Lawrence (225-258 CE) was overseeing the material goods of the Church and distributed alms to the poor in Rome, the then Roman Empire.

When the prefect of Rome wanted to lay his hands on the treasures of the Church, Lawrence distributed them as alms to the poor.

The prefect was furious and had a large gridiron (a type of cooking grill) prepared with hot coals beneath it, and had Lawrence placed on it, hence Lawrence's association with the gridiron on all icons.

After the martyr had suffered for hours, the legend says, he happily declared: "I'm well done on this side. Turn me over!"

St Lawrence is patron saint of cooks, chefs, and comedians.

23.

In November 2019, Croatian police mistakenly deported two Nigerian sportsmen, thinking they were illegal migrants.

24.

The Gadhimai festival in southern Nepal is a sacrificial ceremony held every five years at the Gadhimai Temple of Bariyarpur, in the Bara District,
160 km (100 mi) south of the capital Kathmandu.
The event involves the massive sacrificial slaughter of animals including water buffaloes, pigs, goats, chickens, and pigeons – with the goal of pleasing Gadhimai, the goddess of power.
It is estimated that 50,000 animals were sacrificed during the Gadhimai festival of 2009.

25.

Brazil has a quota for black people when applying for a place in university or when aspiring for a position within the public civil services.
Due to misuse of this "positive discrimination" in the past by white people who had stated they were black in the application forms, now there is a state-funded commission that decides who is black enough to qualify for the quota.

26.

In 2016, the Malaysian government banned yellow
clothing after tens of thousands of protesters wearing
yellow T-shirts flooded the streets of Kuala Lumpur and
demanded the resignation of the Prime Minister.
Since then, anyone wearing yellow can be arrested under
the assumption that they are protesters.

27.

In the US state of Minnesota, pharmacists can turn away patients seeking emergency contraceptives because of religious or personal objection.

28.

Rice Christian is the term used to describe a person who has converted to Christianity for material benefits rather than for religious reasons.

The expression was broadly used in several Asian countries, such as India, Bangladesh, China, Vietnam, and Japan.

The practice was broadly criticized because people in these situations are only formally converting to Christianity in order to receive money or food.

One of the earliest mentions appeared in 1689 when William Dampier wrote regarding the French priests' effort to convert people in Vietnam that "alms of rice have converted more than their preaching".

29.

In 2019, Dutch police found a family living in a basement of a farmhouse in the Drenthe province "waiting for the end of time". A father and his six children had spent over nine years there without any contact with the outside world.

30.

In Iceland, it was legal to kill Basques (inhabitants of the Basque region of Spain) in the period 1615-2015.
The decree was issued in 1615 after a storm destroyed three Basque whaling vessels on an expedition in Icelandic waters.
Eighty members of the crew survived and had to remain in the area. Having nothing to eat, they resorted to robbing people and farmers. The hostilities between locals and the whalers prompted then-sheriff Ari Magnússon to take action. He issued a proclamation that allowed Basques to be killed with impunity in the district. In the month that followed, more than thirty Basques were killed by the sheriff and local farmers.

31.

"The Complete Manual of Suicide" is a Japanese book written by Wataru Tsurumi. First published in 1993, it sold well above one million copies.

He elaborated on the problem of "hardness of living" in Japanese society. In the postscript, Tsurumi claims that he is not encouraging anyone to commit suicide but is merely providing information on how one could escape from the pain, should living become too hard or seem pointless.

32.

The word "*thug*" dates from the 14th century.

Thugs were an extensive criminal network that was active on all main roads in India.

Their modus operandi was to befriend travellers along the roads, gain the travellers' trust, and then murder them by strangulation, and steal their money.

33.

In 1999, the Eastlake region of Oakland,
California (USA), was an area suffering from widespread
criminal activity. It changed when a local resident,
Dan Stevenson, installed in front of his house a Buddha
figurine he had bought from a hardware stall.
In the next few years, the area enjoyed an 82% drop in
criminal incidents. Stevenson, not a religious man
himself, installed the statue just to see what would
happen. The outcome surprised everybody: residents
stopped dumping trash, graffiti disappeared, and drug
dealing in the area plummeted. Even the local prostitutes
moved their business elsewhere.

34.

"Gone with the Wind" is a novel by Margaret Mitchell, first published in 1936. The story is set in Georgia, during the American Civil War and Reconstruction Era.
In the last years, many US schools removed the book from their curricula because Scarlett's second husband was a Ku Klux Klan member.

35.

In Ostritz, Germany, there is a Neo-Nazi rock festival organized every year. In 2019, the police banned alcohol during the event.
Local citizens had contributed by literally buying all the alcohol from supermarkets so that there was not a single bottle available when the Neo-Nazis came to their town.

36.

Until 2018, the US states Idaho and Utah did not allow breastfeeding in public.

37.

In 2018, British pianist, James Rhodes, put a video of himself playing Bach on Facebook. Sony Music Entertainment claimed to own 47 seconds of that performance and, as a result, Facebook muted the video. Johann Sebastian Bach was a German composer and musician of the Baroque period who died in 1750, many years before US copyright law even existed. After the story went viral, Sony dropped this particular claim.

38.

In 2018, a British woman, Freda Jackson, then aged 81, claimed her holiday was ruined because her hotel had "too many Spaniards in it" and that "Spanish people should go somewhere else for their holidays". She had a vacation in Benidorm, Spain.

39.

Sarah Rector (1902-1967) was an African American member of the Muscogee Nation, best known for being the "Richest coloured girl in the world".

In 1913, drillers struck oil on her property and she started to receive a daily income of $300.

Given her wealth, the Oklahoma Legislature declared her to be a white person. This meant she would be allowed to travel first-class on the railroad, among many other privileges.

40.

In 2018, Tokyo Medical University, a prestigious medical school in Japan, confessed to marking down the test scores of female applicants to keep the ratio of women in each class below 30%.

This systematic discrimination, university officials admitted, had started in 2006.

41.

US baseball was segregated until 15 April 1947 when Jackie Robinson became the first African American player to compete in Major League Baseball for the Brooklyn Dodgers.

Robinson broke the colour taboo in a sport that had been segregated for over fifty years.

42.

Obese tourists are crippling the donkeys that carry them around the Greek island of Santorini.

This has forced locals to use mules instead because the latter are sturdier.

43.

In the "distant" 2019, Catholic priests in Poland burned books they considered to be sacrilegious, including ones from the Harry Potter boy wizard series.

44.

A British supermarket chain apologised to Asma Mohiuddin, an expecting mother, for having issued her a parking ticket for "wrongly" using a parent and child parking spot. The incident happened in early 2016, while she was nine months pregnant.

45.

In 2018, a team of 33 researchers published a paper in a peer-reviewed scientific journal, Progress in Biophysics and Molecular Biology, asserting that octopuses are in fact aliens from outer space.
They claim that the Cambrian explosion – a sudden burst of life that happened some 540 million years ago – was the result of extra-terrestrial intervention.

46.

On 16 February 1568, the Spanish Inquisition issued a
death sentence to all residents of the Netherlands.

47.

In 2011, the University of British Columbia conducted a
study in the United States and found that believers
distrusted atheists as much they did rapists.
The study also showed that atheists had lower
employment prospects.

48.

The words "*cannibal*" and "*Caribbean*" have a similar
etymology: from Spanish "*Canibales (plural)*", variant of
Caribes, the name of a West Indian people known
to eat humans.

49.

"Famadihana" is a funerary tradition in Madagascar.
During this ceremony, aka "the turning of the bones", the
Malagasy people retrieve their ancestors' bodies from the

tomb, wrap the corpses in new cloth and rewrite their names on the cloth lest the deceased be forgotten. They dance while carrying the dead above their heads before returning the remains to the family crypts (see photo).

This practice was proven to facilitate pneumonic plague transmission in the region. The Malagasy government has forbidden Famadihana for people who died of plague, but some families are ignoring this decree.

50.

The US state of Delaware abolished flogging as
a legal punishment in 1972.
It had been last used in 1952, when a wife-beater got
20 lashes.

51.

In 2019, the US Department of Agriculture listed
"Wakanda", the fictional nation of Marvel superhero
movie Black Panther, as a free-trade agreement partner in
a bureaucratic mishap.

52.

India's parliament approved in mid-2019 a law that
makes the Muslim practice of "instant divorce"
a criminal offence.
"Triple talaq", as it is known, permits a husband to
divorce his wife by simply repeating the word "*talaq*"
(divorce) three times in any form, including email or
text message. Men violating the new law can be jailed
for up to three years.

53.

In 1892, the Bellamy salute was salute introduced by Francis Bellamy, the author of the American Pledge of Allegiance, as the gesture which was to go along with the pledge. Several decades later, Italian fascists and German Nazis adopted a salute which was quite similar, and which was derived from the Roman salute, a gesture that was broadly (albeit erroneously) believed to have been used in Ancient Rome. This sparked controversy over the use of the Bellamy salute in the United States. It was formally replaced by the hand-over-heart salute when the Congress voted an amendment to the Flag Code on 22 December 1942.

54.

In Iran, men are prohibited from having jagged hairstyles, body tattoos, solarium treatments, or having their eyebrows plucked.

Additionally, men cannot wear necklaces, earrings, neckties, or bright clothing.

55.

In 2019, hundreds of police officers in Jerusalem, Israel, backed up by officers on horseback tried to disperse an ultra-Orthodox street protest.

They received unexpected help from a few women who exposed their breasts, driving away the protesters, who are religiously forbidden from looking at naked women.

56.

In April 2019, Serbia advised its citizens to avoid travelling to the United Kingdom due to "major political chaos", linked to the so-called Brexit, the withdrawal of the UK from the European Union.

57.

On 16 October 1901, for the first time in the US history,
an African American was invited for a dinner by
a sitting US President.

Theodore Roosevelt invited his adviser, spokesman
Booker T. Washington – who was a former slave – to
dine with him and his family.

This attracted waves of criticism from southern
politicians and press.

As a result, no other African American attended a dinner
in the White House for almost thirty years.

58.

Jesús Malverde (literally translating to *Jesus Evilgreen*) –
born as Jesús Juarez Mazo (1870-1909), aka the "Cjuba
Lord", "angel of the poor", or the "narco-saint" – is a
folklore hero in the Mexican state of Sinaloa.

He is celebrated as a saint by some in Mexico and the
United States, basically among drug traffickers.

59.

In 1959, a librarian in Lake City, South Carolina (USA), called the police when a 9-year-old black child named Ronald McNair refused to leave a segregated library without being allowed to check out his books.

McNair completed a PhD in physics from Massachusetts Institute of Technology and became an astronaut.

He died aboard the space shuttle, Challenger.

The library that refused to give him books is now named after him.

60.

Mani Manithan from Tirupattur, India, was 21 years old on 14 June 1989, the last day he ever made a step in the forward-facing direction.

Manithan has spent over three decades walking backwards, believing his peaceful protest would eventually lead the world to harmony.

Walking in reverse, on many occasions fully naked, is his way to protest against global violence and bloodshed.

61.

In 2017, Saudi Arabia accidentally printed a textbook
showing the Star Wars character Yoda sitting next to
King Faisal as he signed the UN charter.

62.

According to a 2020 study conducted by the Saudi Grains
Organization, more than one third of food is wasted in
Saudi Arabia, costing the Kingdom over $10 billion
annually. The country is considered to have the highest
percentage of food waste worldwide.

63.

In 1824, the future US President Andrew Jackson both won the popular vote and received the most votes in the Electoral College, but lost the election anyway.

All four main candidates for the presidency were from the Democratic-Republican Party: Secretary of State John Quincy Adams, Secretary of the Treasury William Harris Crawford, Speaker of the House Henry Clay, and Tennessee Senator Andrew Jackson.

At the time, to win the presidency one needed 131 Electoral College votes. Jackson received 99 votes, Adams – 84, Crawford and Clay – 41 and 37, respectively. As no one reached 131, the election was delegated to the House of Representatives.

As a result of an alleged "Corrupt Bargain" between Clay and Adams, the latter won.

Jackson eventually won the 1828 election, when he defeated the incumbent John Quincy Adams.

64.

According to a 2005 study, 41% of people in the USA
believe in extrasensory perception, also called
the sixth sense, 32% in ghosts, 25% in astrology,
and 21% in communication with the dead.

65.

In 2018, in a weird sort of protest of US sanctions
causing the Turkish currency to plummet, hundreds of
Turks smashed their iPhones and posted videos on
social media.

66.

Most college-age Americans cannot find the UK
on the map.

67.

In Japan, late-night dancing was illegal
in the period 1948-2015.

68.

Robert Lane from New York, USA, named his two sons "Winner" and "Loser".

Winner grew up to be a criminal and Loser became a detective with the police.

69.

In Australia, 11 November 2019 was the driest day since weather records began 137 years earlier.

Every region of the country had virtually zero rainfall.

70.

North Korea's embassy in Germany hosted on its grounds a hotel – City Hostel Berlin.

The tourists who used to sleep there were technically visiting North Korea without leaving Berlin.

The city authorities shut down the hostel in early 2020 because the payment of rent to Pyongyang was in breach of UN sanctions.

71.

A cemetery in Culiacán, Mexico, has many two-story tombs fitted with living rooms, air conditioning, and bulletproof glass. Dedicated to deceased drug lords, some graves cost up to half a million dollars.

72.

The Stalin Monument in the Hague, the Netherlands, is a controversial art object. The conceptual bust of the notorious tyrant, Joseph Stalin, was created in 1986 by Vitaly Komar and Alexander Melamid.
Stalin's bust is placed in a phone booth and has been vandalized many times.

73.

Tulip mania was a period in the Dutch Golden Age
during which prices for bulbs of the recently introduced
tulip reached astronomically high levels and then
plummeted in February 1637.

In 1635, a sale of forty bulbs for 100,000 florins was
recorded.

To give you an idea, a ton of butter cost 100 florins,
a skilled labourer might earn about 300 florins a year.

According to the International Institute of Social History,
one florin in 1637 had the purchasing power of
€11.5 ($13) in 2016.

Tulip mania reached its apogee during the winter of
1636-37, when some bulbs were re-sold dozens of times
in a single day.

It is broadly considered the first recorded
speculative bubble.

74.

In the United States of America, impeachment is the process by which a legislature can charge a civil officer of the government for crimes. The Federal House of Representatives can impeach any federal official, including the President, and each state's legislature can impeach state officials, including the governor. So far, several federal judges have been convicted and removed, but not a single US President.

75.

It is illegal for supermarkets in France to throw away or destroy unsold food.
Since 2016, they have been required to donate any nearly expired food to charities and food banks.
In early 2020, France banned designer clothes and luxury goods companies from destroying unsold or returned items.
The ground-breaking law also covers electrical items, hygiene products and cosmetics, which must now be reused, redistributed or recycled.

76.

Olive Ann Oatman (1837-1903) was a Mormon woman who was kidnapped in 1853 by Native Americans and enslaved for a year.

She was later traded to the Mohave people. Oatman spent four years with them and was treated as a member of the tribe. She became very famous in the 1860s, mostly due to the blue tattooing of her face by the Mohave. Oatman was considered the first known tattooed American woman on record, and her story inspired numerous novels and movies.

77.

Theresa Kachindamoto is the chief of the Dedza District in central Malawi.

She uses her informal authority over one million people to dissolve thousands of child marriages and to promote education for both girls and boys.

78.

In the UK, when Queen Elizabeth II delivers a speech in Parliament, a member of the Parliament is held hostage in Buckingham Palace.

The now ceremonial tradition dates back the reign of King Charles I, whose bad relationship with the Parliament ultimately led to his beheading in 1649.

The "hostage" MP, usually the Vice Chamberlain of the Royal Household, is kept at at Buckingham Palace from the time of the monarch's departure until their return, at which point the hostage is released.

79.

In 1975, the residents of the small coal-mining
town of Vulcan, West Virginia (USA), were isolated
from the outer world when the only bridge out of their
town collapsed.

For almost two years, the state authorities had been
refusing to finance the construction of a new bridge,
which prompted the mayor of Vulcan to request foreign
aid from the Soviet Union and East Germany.

The Soviets readily sent journalists to investigate.

Embarrassed by the Soviet visit to Vulcan,
the West Virginia Legislature promptly sent $1.3 million
for a new bridge.

80.

During WWII, in 1943 pre-sliced bread was banned for a
while in the USA. Bakeries were also obliged to sell
bread at least 12 hours stale.

The government thought these measures would lower
bread consumption.

81.

The term "*hypocognition*" was first used by
US psychiatrist and anthropologist Robert Levy in his
1973 book "Tahitians: Mind and Experience in
the Society Islands".
After studying them for over two years, Levy described
Tahitians as having no words to express sorrow or guilt,
resulting in those who had suffered personal losses
describing themselves as feeling sick or strange
instead of sad.
Levy claimed that their lack of notions for thinking about
and expressing grief correlated with Tahitians' high
suicide rate.

82.

Russian doping is distinct from that in other countries
because the Russian state supplies steroids to athletes.
In 2019, following a myriad of violations, the World
Anti-Doping Agency banned Russia from all major
sporting events for four years.

83.

The first actor to refuse an Oscar Award was
George C. Scott – he rejected his Best Actor Award for
the 1970 film, Patton.
Marlon Brando won Best Actor Oscar for his role in
The Godfather in 1973.
He was the first actor to send someone to reject an Oscar
in person: Brando did not attend the official ceremony
and sent instead an Apache actress named
Sacheen Littlefeather to reject it for him.

84.

The Conch Republic is a micro-nation declared as a
facetious secession of the city of Key West, Florida, from
the United States of America on 23 April 1982.
On that day, Mayor Wardlow proclaimed himself Prime
Minister of the new nation, declared war against the
USA, surrendered after one minute, and requested one
billion dollars in foreign aid for war relief.

This original form of protest was provoked by a US Border Patrol roadblock and checkpoint that infuriated residents and tourists.

The micro-nation is a tourism booster for the city: passports are still issued as collectibles and the "country" has several consulates abroad.

It is noteworthy that during the American Civil War, while Florida seceded and joined the Confederate States of America, Key West remained in the US Union.

85.

The UK Royal family follow some weird rules.
Among the least known are that they cannot play
Monopoly, cannot eat shellfish, and every royal bride
should carry myrtle in her wedding bouquet.

86.

In China, cinema employees flash a laser beam at anyone
texting in the dark.
When ushers spot a lighted mobile phone, they aim a
laser pointer (usually red or green) at the glowing screen.

87.

In 2019, Japan Airlines launched a new seat map for
passengers booking a flight which features a "child icon",
flagging the seats which have already been booked for
infants and babies.

88.

In 2017, Munir Zanial, a Malaysian engineer and permanent resident in the USA, organised a party at a recreational lake in the city of Wichita in Kansas. The property owners saw a Malaysian flag, thought it was "an American flag desecrated with ISIS symbols", and reported Zanial to the security services.

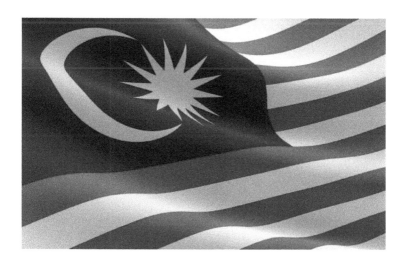

89.

In 2014, 11% of Americans thought that HTML was a type of sexually transmitted disease.

90.

Joshua David Bell (born in 1967) is a famous US violinist and conductor.

In an experiment designed by The Washington Post, Bell played as an incognito street performer at the Metro subway station L'Enfant Plaza in Washington, DC, on 12 January 2007.

The experiment was recorded by a hidden camera; of the 1,097 people who passed by, seven stopped to listen, and one recognized him.

For his nearly 45-minute performance, Bell received $32.17 (approximately €29) from 27 commuters.

Three days before, he had made considerably more playing the same repertoire at a concert, where a ticket cost around 100 dollars (€90).

CHAPTER IV

Animals and plants involved

1.

Have you ever heard of a two-headed snake?
The mysterious disorder is called dicephalus, occurring in just one out of every 100,000 snakes born in the wild and one out of 10,000 born in captivity.

Affected snakes possess two brains with distinct personalities, though one head typically dominates the other, which might lack a trachea, oesophagus, or even eyes.

2.

Roses are more susceptible to the same type of fungal
disease (e.g. powdery mildew, downy mildew)
than the grapevine.
The roses grown in vineyards serve as an early warning
sign to the vineyard manager to take action before the
grapevines get infected.

3.

Obese dog owners are twice as probable to raise
obese dogs.

4.

Worms frozen for 40,000 years in Siberian permafrost
can come back to life.
A 2018 research showed that in Siberia, Russia, melting
permafrost is releasing nematodes – microscopic worms
that live in soil – that have been kept in a deep freeze
since the Pleistocene.
Despite being frozen for so long, two species of these
worms were successfully revived.

5.

Choose your pet smartly: having a snake as a pet could be good for the environment and your carbon footprint.
A snake eats on average ten times less meat than a cat.

6.

Dogs can notice epileptic seizures up to 45 minutes before they occur.
Thanks to their incredible noses,
new research shows, dogs can smell odour molecules in the parts-per-trillion range, including those the human body releases during a seizure.

7.

Cockroaches find humans to be very disgusting.
When they see a human, cockroaches run away as quickly as possible, and if touched by a human, they wash themselves.

8.

Several bird species in the Northern Territory of
Australia, collectively referred to as "firehawks", start
fires intentionally in order to make food collection easier.
Firehawks take sticks already burning from a wildfire and
drop them in another area, which sets a new fire.
As small mammals and insects race to escape the flames
and smoke, they become easy prey for the raptors.

9.

Rabbits and hares eat their own poop and digest it a second time.

In fact, bunnies make two different sorts of droppings: little black round ones and softer ones known as *cecotropes*, the ones that are eaten.

The cecotropes are produced by the fermentation of the food in the *cecum*, a part of the intestinal tract of a rabbit. They are only produced at night, so a rabbit can be seen eating them late at night or early in the morning.

10.

Chick culling or unwanted chick killing is the separating and killing of unwanted (male) chicks, for which the animal farming industry has no use.

It is done in all industrialised egg production, whether free-range, organic, or battery cage.

Worldwide, more than 6 billion male chicks are culled every year in the egg industry.

11.

The Tower of London, officially Her Majesty's Royal Palace and Fortress of the Tower of London, is a historic castle located in central London, UK.

A group of at least six captive ravens live there and they are believed to protect the Crown and the Tower.

According to a superstition "if the Tower of London ravens are lost or fly away, the Crown will fall and Britain with it".

There is even a full-time position of a keeper, titled the Ravenmaster of the Yeomen Warders, who is tasked to maintain the welfare of the ravens of the Tower of London.

12.

In 2018, after her calf's death, an orca mother carried its cadaver with her for over a week across hundreds of kilometres.

13.

Canaries were extensively used in coalmines to detect the presence of carbon monoxide.

Their rapid breathing rate, small size, and high metabolism, led birds in dangerous mines to succumb much faster, thereby giving the miners time to escape.

14.

The suicide plant, *Dendrocnide moroides* –
aka the stinging brush, mulberry-leaved stinger,
gympie stinger, or moonlighter – is a plant indigenous
to rainforest areas in Indonesia and the north-eastern
regions of Australia.

When touched, it can deliver multiple stings with a
long-lasting neurotoxin that is extremely painful.

Some people would rather kill themselves than live
through days of excruciating pain, and then
years of lesser pain.

If the microscopic hairs that deliver the stings are not
extracted, the pain can continue for several years.

The pain, which has been described like being dipped
in hot acid and being electrocuted at the same time, is
reported to be so excruciating that injured individuals
have been driven mad by it and have resorted
to suicide.

Horses stung by this plant have literally thrown
themselves off cliffs.

15.

The *chupacabra* (Spanish for *"goat-sucker"*) is a legendary folklore creature in parts of the Americas, with its first purported sightings in Puerto Rico. The name comes from the animal's reported habit of attacking and drinking the blood of livestock, including goats.

16.

Every day, over 35 million chickens are slaughtered for food in the USA alone.
The average life span of a broiler is 6-8 weeks.
In contrast, cock fighters live for at least two years.

17.

A positive piece of news: in 2003, US shelters in New York City killed more than two-thirds of the dogs and cats they took in.
As of 2016, the proportion was down to 13%.

18.

San-nakji is a variety of Korean raw dishes made with

long arm octopus (*Octopus minor*).

The octopuses are put to death before being cut into small

pieces and served, but the nerve activity in the octopus'

tentacles makes the pieces move posthumously on the

plate whilst served.

19.

A Polish environmental group, EcoLogic Group, was

using a mobile-phone transmitter to track migratory

movements of a stork in 2017-18.

The bird went missing in Sudan and someone started

using the SIM card to make calls.

In 2018, EcoLogic received a phone bill of

10,000 zlotys ($2,650; €2,400).

20.

Globally, cats kill billions of birds every year and have

led to the extinction of at least thirty-three bird species.

21.

Fleas and ticks on numerous animal species transmit the highly virulent strains of the plague bacterium, *Yersinia pestis*.

Those include grey marmots, rock squirrels, wood rats, ground squirrels, prairie dogs, chipmunks, mice, voles, and rabbits.

Additionally, wild carnivores can contract the plague by eating infected animals.

22.

In June 2014, a plane crashed on a routine trip across the Congo.

The pilot, co-pilot, and seventeen passengers perished, leaving only one survivor to tell his incredible story.

Apparently, a passenger had smuggled a live crocodile onto the flight in his hand luggage, and when the reptile escaped, commotion ensued.

Crew and passengers rushed to the front of the aircraft, dangerously shifting the plane's centre of weight and throwing it off balance, leading to the fatal crash.

23.

The shoebill (*Balaeniceps rex*) aka whalehead, whale-headed stork, or shoe-billed stork, is a remarkably large stork-like bird. As its name suggests, it has an enormous shoe-shaped bill.

Shoebills seldom raise more than one chick but will hatch more. The younger chicks often die and serve as "back-ups" just in case the eldest chick dies or is weak.

24.

A 2014 study claimed that domestic cats have the urge to kill humans and would do so, if only they were larger.

25.

In 2018, Texan Jeremy Sutcliffe was bitten by the severed head of a rattlesnake and needed twenty-six doses of anti-venom.

He saw the serpent in his garden and decapitated it. When Sutcliffe took the snake's remains to dispose of them, the head bit him.

A snake's bite reflex can remain active up to several hours after death.

26.

In early 2020, wildlife rangers killed one of Kenya's emblematic animals, Mohawk the lion.

A group of men had approached the lion in the town of Isinya, near the capital Nairobi. At first, they took pictures. Then they approached the wildcat and started throwing rocks and sticks at him. Finally, Mohawk attacked one of the teasers.

Unfortunately, the animal management team that first arrived had no tranquilizers, only hunting rifles.

27.

The quokka (*Setonix brachyurus*) is a marsupial about the size of a domestic cat.

Quokkas are mainly nocturnal and, like kangaroos and other members in the macropod family, they are herbivorous and do not need a lot of water to survive. They are notorious for their survival instinct: if a quokka mother is threatened by a predator, she will often throw her baby on the ground to distract the predator and save her own life.

28.

In 2017, a UK angler nearly died when he accidentally
swallowed a fish he had just caught.
Sam Quilliam stopped breathing and had a cardiac arrest
after the 14 cm (5.5 in)-long Dover sole jumped out of his
hand and "swam down" his throat.
He wanted to kiss the fish in celebration of his catch
on Boscombe Pier, Bournemouth,
when the accident occurred.
Paramedics managed to retrieve the fish from his throat
with forceps.

29.

In 2013, millipedes caused a train crash in Australia.
A train entering a station in the town of Clarkson ended
up hitting a train that was parked at the station.
The authorities blamed "lots of millipedes being squished
at the same time on the tracks leading to much less
friction than normal".

30.

In the distant past, elephant birds were abundant in Madagascar. They weighed at least half a tonne, were up to 3 m (10 ft) tall and laid giant eggs.

They became extinct in the 13th century, most probably as a result of human activity.

31.

Every hour, thousands of sharks are caught and killed. Many shark species are the victims of culling in attempts to make beaches safer, trophy catches, bycatch by commercial fishing boats, and the malicious practice of finning for food.

32.

To suck more blood, mosquitoes filter out and excrete part of the water it contains.

Eliminating the water lets them take in up to ten times more blood than they otherwise could.

33.

Irma Bule, an Indonesian pop singer known for
performing with live snakes, died in 2016 after
a King Cobra attacked her during a concert.

34.

Giving cats food containing an antibody may help people
with cat allergies.

Pet food maker, Purina, is examining how adding an
antibody to the pet food prevents reactions in the owners.

35.

A chemical compound called *"castoreum"* is used in flavoured foods (mostly ice creams) as a substitute for vanilla. As its name suggests, it is extracted from beavers (*genus Castor*).

More precisely, from beavers' anal glands.

36.

Vulture bees are three closely related North American stingless bee species in the *genus Trigona* that eat rotting meat.

They substitute meat for pollen, but still produce honey.

This shocking behaviour was only discovered in 1982, two centuries after these insects were first classified.

37.

In 2019, California became the first US state to ban animal fur products.

Leather and some animal skins are still allowed, while circuses are prohibited from using wild animals like lions, tigers, and bears.

38.

You can visually distinguish between orcas
(killer whales) born and living in captivity, and their
wild siblings.
The dorsal fin of wild orcas is upright, while those born
in captivity have a dorsal fin bent to one side.

39.

According to a study published by the UK Royal Society, the population of humpback whales is in recovery after it was on the brink of extinction due to centuries of human over-exploitation.

Western South Atlantic humpbacks were reduced to a several hundred individuals in the 1950s, after once numbering over 27,000.

However, efforts to preserve the animal have paid off, with current numbers estimated around 25,000 – about 94% of their pre-exploitation levels.

40.

The western mosquitofish (*Gambusia affinis*), also known simply as mosquitofish, is a freshwater fish species. They are small in comparison to many other freshwater species, with females reaching a maximum length of 7 cm (2.8 in) and males – 4 cm (1.6 in).

This fish eats mosquito larvae (hence the name "*mosquitofish*") and has been used more than any other species for the biological control of mosquitoes.

From the 1920s to the 1950s, mosquitofish were considered a key factor in eradicating malaria in South America, southern Russia, and Ukraine.
A very famous example of that is the coast of the Black Sea near Sochi (Russia), where the mosquitofish is commemorated for eradicating malaria by a statue.

41.

Besides the actual bird, a black swan could denote a phenomenon that comes as a surprise as it was not predicted or was very hard to predict.

When it is applied to the stock market, black swan is typically something negative. Examples of financial black swan events include the dot-com bubble of 2001, the 9/11 terrorist attacks, and, more recently, the COVID-19 pandemic of 2020. The term stems from the fact that Europeans thought all swans were white before they first saw an Australian black swan – *cygnus atratus*.

CHAPTER V

Wars and military action

1.

In 1918, Quentin Roosevelt – a World War I pilot in the United States Air Service and the fourth son of former US President Theodore Roosevelt – was shot down and killed by a German Fokker plane in France. The German Army buried him with full military honours.

2.

Sir William Wallace (1270-1305) was a Scottish knight and one of the main leaders during the First War of Scottish Independence. Wallace is famous for having defeated an English army at the Battle of Stirling Bridge in September 1297.

It all ended in August 1305, when he was captured, hanged, drawn and quartered for high treason, as graphically shown in the Oscar-winning film, Braveheart.

By the way, "*Wallace*" means "*Welshman*".

3.

Los Alamos, New Mexico (USA), was the site of Project Y, the top-secret atomic weapons laboratory managed by J. Robert Oppenheimer.

The site was so top secret that just one mailbox, PO Box 1663, served as the mailing address for the entire town.

Hundreds of children born there had on their birth certificates "PO Box 1663" as a birthplace.

4.

Historically, when someone died on a ship in wartime,
they were given burial at sea.
Nowadays, it is typically possible to airlift the corpse
back to shore and hold a burial ceremony on land.
However, as recently as the Falklands War (in 1982),
the deceased soldiers were buried at sea
without returning to land.

5.

In October 1883, the Spanish town of Líjar declared war
on France requesting the French government to formally
apologize to Spanish King Alfonso XII, who had been
treated with disrespect during a visit to Paris.
Líjar warned "the inhabitants of the French Territory"
that the town had "six hundred useful men" capable,
each of them, to kill 10,000 French soldiers.
Without any bloodshed, one hundred years later, on
30 October 1983, the peace treaty was solemnly signed
by the political and military authorities
of the opposing sides.

6.

Between 1809 and 1981, the town of Huéscar, Spain, was formally at war with Denmark as a result of the Napoleonic wars over Spain in the early 19th century, when Denmark supported the French Empire.
This official declaration of war had been forgotten until a local historian discovered it in 1981.
The city mayor and the Ambassador of Denmark signed a peace treaty on 11 November 1981.
Nobody was killed or injured during the 172 years of war.

7.

Harold Joseph "Harry" Greene (1959-2014) was a US Army general who lost his life during the War in Afghanistan.
At the rank of major general, Greene was the highest-ranking US officer killed by enemy action since the Vietnam War.

8.

Vice-Admiral Horatio Nelson (1758-1805) was a British flag officer in the Royal Navy, known for a number of decisive British naval victories, particularly during the Napoleonic Wars.

In 1805, he was shot and killed during his victory at the Battle of Trafalgar and his body was placed in a barrel of brandy mixed with camphor and myrrh.

9.

The German-Soviet campaign during World War II
(WWII) accounted for five times as many deaths as all
the other European combat theatres combined.

10.

During WWII, self-inflicted losses in the Soviet Red
Army were higher than all US soldiers killed in action.

11.

On 16 June 1941, when the defeat of France by the
German Army was impending, the United Kingdom
proposed the creation of the Franco-British Union.
The constitution of the Union foresaw joint organs of
defence, foreign, financial and economic policies.
Every citizen of France would instantly receive UK
citizenship, and every British subject would become,
in turn, a citizen of France.
France refused and surrendered to Germany.

12.

During WWII, the notorious SS soldiers had a tattoo on
their left arm indicating their blood type.
It was meant to save their lives in case of wounding, but
in reality helped their identification
(and indictment) after the war.

13.

In the early 20th century, the German Empire developed
military plans to invade the USA.
None of them was feasible.

14.

The Republic of Ireland was the only British Dominion
that did not support the UK during WWII.
Ireland maintained its neutrality, but in 1940 experienced
several German bombing raids.
In 1943, the German government paid
a compensation of £9,000 (worth today approximately
£413,000, €450,000 or $500,000).

15.

In 2009, Somali pirates created a "stock exchange" to
fund their hijacking operations.
Any Somali civilian can invest in one of seventy
"maritime companies" and hope that their chosen pirate
band gets rich with the successful ransoming of a
captured ship and crew.
People do not even need to invest cash –
rocket launchers, assault rifles, and other weapons are
also accepted.

16.

The Moroccan Western Sahara Wall is a 2,700 km
(1,700 mi)-long structure, mainly a sand wall
(or "berm"), through Western Sahara and
the south-western portion of Morocco.
It separates the Moroccan-occupied and controlled areas
(the Southern Provinces) on the west from the Polisario-
controlled zone (Free Zone, or Sahrawi Arab Democratic
Republic) on the east.
The fortifications consist of sand and stone walls about
3 m (10 ft) in height, with bunkers, fences, and countless
landmines along them.
The barrier mine belt along the structure is thought to be
the longest continuous minefield
in the world.

17.

2016 was the first year since 1968 when no British
soldiers died in a military operation.

18.

Biological weapons have been used since antiquity.
During the 1346 siege of Caffa, a well-fortified Genoese-controlled seaport (now Feodosia, Ukraine), the attacking Mongol force were struck by an epidemic of plague.
Attackers started catapulting the cadavers of their dead into the besieged city, thus sparkling a plague epidemic in Caffa.

The retreating Genoese forces spread the infection across Europe. The plague pandemic that followed, aka the Black Death, ravaged through Europe, the Near East, and North Africa and was probably the most devastating public health disaster in recorded history.

19.

USS Pueblo is a research ship, used by the US Navy intelligence as a spy ship. It was detained by North Korean forces on 23 January 1968 in what is known today as the "Pueblo Incident".

The capture of Pueblo and the torture of her crew during the subsequent 11-month captivity became an important Cold War incident, increasing tensions between Western and Eastern powers.

The captured American crewmembers ruined North Korea's efforts at propaganda by discreetly giving the finger in staged photo ops.

The North Koreans were not aware what the gesture meant and were at first told by the Americans that it was a "Hawaiian good luck sign", similar to the shaka.

20.

During World War II, the USA developed three prototypes of nuclear weapons:

"Thin Man", named for President Roosevelt, which utilized the plutonium gun design; "Fat Man", named after Winston Churchill, was an implosion prototype; and "Little Boy", named after President Roosevelt's brother was using a lighter, smaller uranium design.

In mid-1944, the "Thin Man" project was abandoned.

21.

Exercise Tiger, aka Operation Tiger, was one of the rehearsals for the D-Day invasion of Normandy, which took place in April 1944 on Slapton Sands in Devon, UK.

Coordination and communication problems caused friendly fire deaths during the exercise, and an Allied convoy preparing itself for the landing was attacked by the German submarines, resulting in the deaths of more than 700 US soldiers.

It was the worst loss of life since the Japanese attack on Pearl Harbor in 1941.

22.

The Battle of Bicocca took place on 27 April 1522,
during the Italian War of 1521-26.

A combined French and Venetian army under
Odet of Foix, Viscount of Lautrec, was annihilated by an
Imperial-Spanish and Papal army under the command of
Prospero Colonna.

In the aftermath, Lautrec withdrew from Lombardy,
leaving the Duchy of Milan in Imperial hands.

French/Swiss forces lost more than 3,000 killed, while
their enemies' casualties were fewer than 200.

Because of the battle, the word "*bicoca*" – meaning *a
bargain* – entered the Spanish language.

In French, on the contrary, it means "*dilapidated house*".

23.

The Treaty of Versailles was the most important of the
peace treaties that ended World War I.

Curiously, among other stipulations, the treaty also
standardised the concert pitch at 435 Hz.

24.

Andrei Nikolayevich Tupolev (1888-1972) was a Soviet aeronautical engineer who participated in the design of more than 100 types of civilian and military aircraft in the Soviet Union for over fifty years.

He was awarded numerous titles and honours (including the Hero of Socialist Labour, the Order of Lenin, and the Order of the Red Banner of Labour) and promoted to the rank of Colonel-General of the Soviet Air Force in 1968.

In 2018, one of Moscow's airports was renamed to Vnukovo Andrei Tupolev International Airport.

However, during the so-called Great Purge he was arrested on made-up charges for espionage, sabotage, and supporting the Russian Fascist Party.

He spent the period 1937-41 behind bars and created in prison one of the most prolific Soviet WWII bombers, Tu-2 (see photo).

25.

The Vietnam War – in Vietnam known as the Resistance
War Against America or simply the American War – was
a major conflict in Vietnam, Laos, and Cambodia from
1955 to 1975. It was the second of the Indochina Wars
and was formally fought between North Vietnam and
South Vietnam.

North Vietnam was assisted by the Soviet Union, China,
and other communist allies; South Vietnam was
supported by the USA, South Korea, the Philippines,
Australia, Thailand, and others.

What you probably do not know is that the USA has
never declared war on Vietnam.

26.

The Janissaries (Turkish: "*yeniçeri*" meaning "new soldier") were elite foot soldiers that made up the Ottoman Sultan's household troops, bodyguards and the first modern standing army in Europe.

The unit was established during the reign of sultan Murad I (1362-1389). It started as an elite corps of slaves formed of kidnapped young Christian boys, such as Bulgarians, Serbs, Greeks, Albanians, and Armenians. These boys were then converted to Islam, and became renowned for their utmost internal cohesion and strict discipline.

Unlike ordinary slaves, they were paid monthly salaries. Forbidden to marry or do business, their absolute loyalty to the Sultan was expected.

Interestingly, they were given a Muslim name upon enlisting, but all of them shared the same family name: Abdullah (son of God).

CHAPTER VI

Sounds like a conspiracy theory or fake news but is not

1.

In New York City, USA, the Grand Central Station
produces more radiation than allowed in
a nuclear power plant.
It gives you a dose of radiation when you go through it
due to the granite used in its construction.

2.

Mehran Karimi Nasseri, aka Sir Alfred Mehran
(born 1946), is an Iranian refugee.
He used to live in the departure lounge of Terminal 1 in
Charles de Gaulle Airport, Paris, France, from 1988 until
2006, when he had to be hospitalized.
In 2004, Nasseri's autobiography was published as a
book, "The Terminal Man", and inspired the 2004
Steven Spielberg film "The Terminal".

3.

Rain can contain vitamin B12.
Many microorganisms that occur naturally in nature
like *Streptomyces* and *Pseudomonas* can produce
vitamin B12.
As you know, rainwater drops are not pure water,
capturing microorganisms as they fall through the air and
wash our rooftops.
Rainwater often contains these B12-producing organisms.

4.

Operation LAC (*Large Area Coverage*) was a US Army Chemical Corps covert operation which sprayed miniscule zinc cadmium sulphide (ZnCdS) particles over a large part of the United States and Canada in order to test dispersal patterns and the maximum range of chemical and biological weapons. In the 1950s, the Army dispersed ZnCdS particles via motorized blowers, from the backs of SUVs, and via airplanes.
Additionally, LAC used *Bacillus globigii* to simulate biological warfare agents (such as anthrax) because, at the time, the bacterium was thought to have negligible health consequence to people; however, it is now considered a human pathogen.

5.

In 1907, French waiters went on strike for the right to have moustaches.
Until then, in France, moustaches were a symbol of class, while waiters were seen as lower class and thus not worthy of sporting a moustache.

6.

In March 2020, oil prices fell so low that, for a moment,
the least attractive sort of oil, Wyoming Asphalt Sour,
was minus $0.19 a barrel.

On 20 April 2020, the price of West Texas Intermediate,
the US crude oil benchmark, was negative for the first
time in history.

Producers were literally paying buyers to take oil
deliveries as storage capacity began to run out.

7.

In New Zealand in the 1930s, farmers reported multiple
occasions of exploding trousers.

Farmers had been spraying sodium chlorate,
a government-recommended weed killer, onto ragwort
(an agricultural weed), and some of the liquid had ended
up on their clothes. Sodium chlorate is a strong oxidizing
agent, and reacted with the organic fibres (i.e. the wool
and the cotton) of the clothes.

Farmers' trousers would burst into flame, especially
when exposed to extreme heat or naked flames.

8.

Frane Selak (born 1929) is a Croatian man who is said to have cheated death seven times and afterward won the lottery jackpot in 2003. Journalists started calling him "the world's luckiest man".

His first brush with death was in January 1962 when his train fell into a river, drowning seventeen passengers. The next year, he survived an airplane crash that killed nineteen. In 1966, a bus that he was riding in plunged into a river, drowning four people. In 1970, his car caught fire as he was driving, but he managed to run away before the fuel tank blew up. Three years later, in another driving incident, the engine of his car burst into flames.

In 1995, he was struck by a bus in Zagreb.

In 1996 he avoided a head-on collision on a mountain curve and his car fell some 90 metres (300 ft) into a gorge; he was ejected from the vehicle and managed to hold onto a tree.

In 2003, right after his 73rd birthday, Selak won €900,000 (US$1.1 million) in the lottery.

9.

In 1940, two identical twin boys were separated at the age of three weeks and adopted by separate families in Ohio, USA.

Thirty-nine years later, the brothers were reunited and found fascinating similarities in virtually every aspect of their lives.

They had both been named James by their adoptive parents. Both worked as law enforcement agents. Both married women named Linda, had a divorce, and then remarried women named Betty. Both had sons named James Allan (or Alan) and a dog named Toy. Both drove a Chevrolet and were heavy smokers.

10.

In 1977, US car manufacturers recalled more cars than they produced.

11.

In 1999, the Grand Duchy of Luxembourg burned 50 billion of a top-secret currency that never entered into circulation: the "new" Luxembourgish franc that was printed in secret as a back-up plan should the newly introduced euro fail.

Immediately after the celebrations on 1 January 1999 as the euro was adopted as the currency in Luxembourg and ten other countries of the European Union, the Luxembourgish Army spent weeks to incinerate the truckloads of banknotes.

These events were revealed some twenty years later by the President of the European Commission, Jean-Claude Juncker, who had served as Luxembourg's finance minister in the 1990s.

12.

The Lord of the Flies happened for real in June 1965.

The protagonists were six boys aged between thirteen and

sixteen – Sione, Stephen, Kolo, David, Luke, and Mano –

all pupils at a strict Catholic boarding school in

Nuku'alofa, Tonga.

They felt bored and created a plan to escape to Fiji, some

800 km (500 mi) away, or even all the way to

New Zealand.

They stole a sailing boat and quickly got lost in the sea as

no-one among them had any sailing experience.

By chance, they landed on the uninhabited island 'Ata,

where, unlike the macabre events in the Lord of the Flies,

they spent in relative harmony over a year.

According to the captain who rescued the boys,

they had set up a small garden and had built improvised

rainwater containers, chicken pens, and even

a badminton court.

(see photo)

13.

A driver from Luxembourg received a fine for exceeding
the speed limits within the Belgian capital, Brussels.
According to the obviously erroneous legal document,
in early 2018 he had driven at 914 km/h (568 mph), while
"after correction, only 859 km/h (534 mph) has been
taken into account for the penalty".

14.

At any given moment, Bitcoin miners are using enough energy to power over two million US homes.

15.

In 2017, US President Donald Trump's Twitter account was temporarily deleted. Twitter described the perpetrator as a "customer support employee who did this on his last day".

CHAPTER VII

Irony, bad luck, and natural disasters

1.

US Senator Rand Paul was the only senator to vote against a bill providing $8.3 billion in emergency funding to deal with coronavirus in March 2020.
A few days later, he became the first known senator to test positive for COVID-19.

2.

The chances of getting killed by rubbish falling from space are estimated 1 in 5 billion.

3.

In the USA, more people die from overdose of synthetic opioids such as fentanyl than there are victims of heroin and cocaine overdoses combined.

4.

US Presidents J. F. Kennedy, Theodore Roosevelt, and Ronald Reagan were all members of The National Rifle Association (NRA) and were all shot at.

5.

In 1915, the SS Eastland disaster killed 844 passengers,
which overshadows the passengers' death toll of
the Titanic (829) and the Lusitania (785), yet almost
no one has even heard of it.

After the Titanic disaster in 1912, regulations required
more rescue boats. Ironically, SS Eastland had far too
many boats on the upper decks and capsized in
the Chicago River.

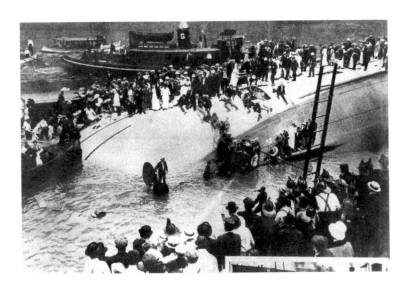

6.

Natural is not always better: natural almond flavour contains traces of cyanide; artificial one does not.

7.

In 2017, a psychic medium, Theprit Palee, died after stabbing himself in the heart during a failed act to prove his immortality in Chiang Mai, northern Thailand.

8.

On 8 January 1992, while attending a banquet hosted by the Prime Minister of Japan, Kiichi Miyazawa, US President George H. W. Bush fainted, after vomiting in Miyazawa's lap.

9.

In 2014, three people using a flight simulator were killed in a plane crash at Wichita's Mid-Continent Airport, Kansas (USA). They died when a twin-engine airplane, whose pilot also perished, crashed into the building of their flight training centre.

10.

In 2018, James Rynerson was mistakenly released from Mesa County Jail, Colorado (USA), due to an identity mix-up. He was there awaiting his trial on threatening, disorderly conduct and trespass charges. Rynerson went straight home to his wife. She was not happy to see him and drove him straight back to jail a couple of hours later.

11.

As of 2020, more than 200 corpses of unlucky climbers have remained on the slopes of Mount Everest.

12.

In poker, the so-called "dead man's hand" is described as a two-pair poker hand consisting of the black aces and black eights. Those were the cards reportedly held by Old West folk hero and gunfighter, Wild Bill Hickok, when he was murdered while playing a game.

13.

Some car manufacturers should have known better when choosing the names for their car models. Some examples: Mazda LaPuta (in Spanish it means: "the whore"), Mitsubishi Pajero (in Spanish: "*wanker*"), Chevrolet Nova (in Spanish: "*It doesn't go*"), Opel Ascona (in Portuguese: "*female genitalia*"), and Honda Fitta (in Swedish and Norwegian: "*cunt*").

14.

In 1997, the song "Ironic" by Alanis Morissette was nominated for a Grammy Award. Ironically, the song's lyrics describe mostly bad luck, and not irony.

15.

In the 1960s, Chilean Tomás Martinez fled to Bolivia to escape prosecution for writing some bad cheques.

In 2000, he was homeless and living on the streets of Santa Cruz de la Sierra, Bolivia, when he run away from approaching police officers.

Unbeknownst to him, they were bringing him news of a $6-million inheritance. Martinez disappeared and has never been found, causing Bolivian newspapers to dub him "the new millionaire paradoxically not knowing his fortune".

16.

A French citizen, fluent in French, was denied a certificate she needed to settle in Canada's French-speaking part, Quebec.

According to the authorities, she had not demonstrated sufficient proficiency in French because one chapter of her doctoral thesis was written in English.

17.

Pompeii was a Roman town in nowadays southern Italy. On 24 August 79 CE, the adjacent volcano, Mount Vesuvius, erupted and buried Pompeii under volcanic ash, killing the vast majority of the inhabitants. The town did experience several earthquakes, which scientists today would recognise as a warning sign of imminent eruption, and in 62 CE there was a massive earthquake that destroyed entire quarters of the town. The inhabitants of Pompeii, however, did not know that Mount Vesuvius was a volcano and, in fact, there even was no word for volcano in Latin. By the way, the word *volcano* is derived from "Vulcan", the Roman God of Fire. Today, Mount Vesuvius remains the only active volcano in mainland Europe.

18.

In the USA, between 9% and 10% of those struck by lightning die, with an annual average of 25 deaths in the last decade.

19.

In 2012, a woman on a visit to Iceland took part in a major mountain search operation for a lost tourist. A few hours later, she realised that she was the missing person everyone was looking for.

20.

In 1986, a hailstorm killed around 100 people in Gopalganj, Bangladesh. The hailstones were the size of grapefruits and weighed up to 1.02 kg (2.25 lb) each.

21.

Earth's magnetic north pole is moving east very fast, shifting from the Canadian Arctic toward Russia. The rapid change of the magnetic poles has impact over navigation, GPS systems, military operations, etc. The northern magnetic pole has been heading toward Russia at a speed of 55 km (34 mi) per year but has slowed recently to 40 km (25 mi) per year.

22.

In 1974, the Licor de Merda (*Liquor of Shit*) was first made in the wine region of Cantanhede, Portugal. It was crafted to "honour" the dictator who then ruled Portugal and does not, in fact, contain excrement.

It started as a joke, but the drink sold well.

Licor de Merda is made with milk, and also contains herbs, sugar, cocoa, cinnamon, and vanilla.

23.

Every minute, on average, two people drown somewhere in the world.

24.

In 2009, the Maldives government made an impressive plea for climate change action by holding the world's first underwater cabinet meeting. The meeting, held at 6 m (20 ft) depth, lasted half an hour and illustrated what the Maldives' future could be. The 350,000 inhabitants of the country live on 1,192 coral islands on average only 2.1 m (7 ft) above the sea level.

25.

Rogue waves (aka freak waves, monster waves, episodic waves, killer waves, extreme waves, and abnormal waves) are extremely large, unpredictable and suddenly appearing surface waves that can be tremendously dangerous, even to large ships such as ocean liners.

A rogue wave was first scientifically recorded on 1 January 1995, when a 26 m (85 ft) wave hit a Norwegian rig, the Draupner platform, at 72 km/h (45 mph).

No one knows for sure how rogue waves are formed.

26.

Almost all ships lost in the 2004 Asian tsunami
were in port.

Tsunamis are nearly unnoticeable in deep water and only
become dangerous as they approach the coast and the
ocean floor becomes shallower; therefore, tsunamis do
not present a threat to shipping at sea.

27.

After the 2004 tsunami, many people in Southeast Asia
stopped eating seafood.

They believe that their relatives who died in the ocean
during the tsunami were eaten by sea creatures and eating
seafood is indirectly cannibalism.

###

VERIFICATION PROCESS

To start with, however a great read Wikipedia is, I have never used it to confirm facts; I instead checked the sources listed there and evaluated them.

Anything science-related like "While only 2% of Europeans lack the gene for smelly armpits, most East Asians and almost all Koreans lack it" would need to be confirmed by at least two (preferably three) separate scientific publications, be it on paper or online of the sort of www.science.gov/, www.nasa.gov/, www.britannica.com/, www.sciencemag.org/, www.newscientist.com/, www.genome.gov/, www.howstuffworks.com/, www.merriam-webster.com/.

The scientific publications and websites of the best universities worldwide are also consistently checked (excerpt from the list): University of Cambridge, Stanford University, University of Oxford, California Institute of Technology, Massachusetts Institute of Technology, Harvard University, Princeton University, Imperial College London, ETH Zurich – Swiss Federal Institute of Technology, Yale University, Columbia University, University of Toronto, Humboldt University of Berlin, University of Tokyo, Heidelberg University, University of Melbourne, Peking University etc.

For events or facts of the type "In the USA, consumption of Corona beer dropped by more than 30% since the start of 2020 pandemic of COVID-19" I checked at least three reputable newspaper articles and confirmed television reports. Example for newspapers/TV channels used to verify events: The New York Times, Washington Post, Wall Street Journal, The Guardian, The Economist, Financial Times, Times of India, Le Monde, The Sydney Morning Herald, Frankfurter Allgemeine Zeitung, Bloomberg, Al Jazeera, Reuters, Associated Press, BBC, TV5 MONDE, CNN, etc.

ACKNOWLEDGEMENTS

This book is dedicated to my family: my loving wife, Anna, my curious and restless sons, Pavel and Nikolay, and my mother, Maria, who sparked my interest in reading. Thank you for being so patient with me during the lengthy process of writing. You are my inspiration!

Many thanks to my editor, Andrea Leitenberger, to all test readers, friends, and colleagues who provided vital feedback and constructive criticism.

ZEALOUS TEST READERS:

Alexandra Oliveira-Jones
Brian Power
Cathy Ciszek
Dimitar Dimitrov
Elaine Fitt
Elijah Zhai
Eva Goulas
Gayle Hoefker
Heather Wilkinson
Istvan Kovacs
Jackie Milne
Jess Bauldry
Kalina Simeonova
Linda Van Ras
Liz Read
Marina Heda
Matthew E. McGoey
Robert Pernetta

ABOUT THE AUTHOR

Born in Bulgaria, I have lived in places like Germany, Belgium, and Iraq, before settling down with my family in Luxembourg. With varied interests, I have always suffered from an insatiable appetite for facts stemming from an unrestrainable intellectual curiosity. It has undoubtedly influenced my academic background and career: after acquiring Master degrees in Greek Philology, German and English Translation, I graduated in Crisis Management and Diplomacy, and most recently undertook an MBA. Member of the high IQ society MENSA.

My career has been equally broad and diverse, swinging from that of an army paratrooper and a military intelligence analyst; through to that of a civil servant with the European Commission, and presently, that of a clerk, performing purely financial tasks in a major bank.

My hobbies include scuba diving, travelling, and learning foreign languages.

CONNECT WITH THE AUTHOR

Email: **n.kostov@raiseyourbrain.com**

Facebook: **www.facebook.com/raiseyourbrain/**

Twitter: **@RaiseYourBrain**

Blog: **www.RaiseYourBrain.com**

Instagram: **www.instagram.com/raiseyourbrain/**

FOLLOW ME ON GOODREADS:

goodreads   Home   My Books   Browse ▾

165 ratings | 33 reviews | avg rating:4.60

more photos (3)

#1 most followed
#45 best reviewers
#2 top librarians
#64 top reviewers

OTHER BOOKS
AVAILABLE ON
AMAZON:

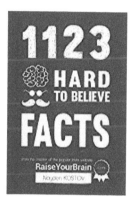

I hope you have enjoyed this book. I would greatly appreciate it if you write your honest **review** on Amazon and/or on GoodReads.com

***

DOWNLOAD A FREE BOOK SAMPLE from my website **RaiseYourBrain.com :**

1123 Hard To Believe Facts

Which Is NOT True? - The Quiz Book

Fascinating Facts for the Whole Family
(Silver medal from 2020 Readers' Favorite Awards)

853 Hard To Believe Facts

523 Hard To Believe Facts

You could also subscribe for my newsletter and learn first about my future projects.

Lightning Source UK Ltd.
Milton Keynes UK
UKHW011457110222
398558UK00002B/505

9 782919 960231